TPR

IS MORE ___
COMMANDS —
AT ALL LEVELS

El_____ ijn

This s_____ ntains
SIGN_____ Story-
telling_____ ription
of "In_____ 5.

Con_____ ute

http://hometo_____ usiness.html

TPR Is More Than Commands
is published by the
Command Performance Language Institute,
which features
Total Physical Response products
and other fine products
related to language acquisition
and teaching.

First published March, 1995
  Second Printing with corrections and additions, February, 1996
Second Edition, August, 1998
  Second Printing with corrections and additions, August, 2001

Illustrations by Cherie Hearne on p. 47 and Christopher Talleck on pp. 55 and 68 used with permission.

Printed in the U.S.A. on 50% recycled, acid-free paper with soy-based ink.

ISBN 0-929724-14-3

Dedicated to all our students.
They have been our greatest teachers.

What we learn with pleasure,
we never forget.

— Alfred Mercier

Contents

Preface

The predecessor of TPR (Total Physical Response) did not have a name. It was apparently born in the early 1920s with the work of Englishman Harold E. Palmer (1877-1949) and his daughter Dorothée in Japan, where he was linguistic advisor to the Ministry of Education in 1922-23 and, from 1923 to 1936, Director of the Institute for Research in English Teaching, a department of the Ministry of Education. They published the first known book, *English through Actions*, about this extraordinary approach to language teaching and learning in Tokyo in 1925. Prior to going to Japan, Palmer had developed what he called his Oral Method while working in Belgium and London. The approach he and his daughter describe in *English through Actions* was evidently integrated into the broader Oral Method (see bibliography for some of his principal works). It seems that his ideas were generally respected in Japan but, for "socio-pedagogical" reasons, were little used by Japanese teachers of English. It is not known to what degree the *English through Actions* approach was used outside of Japan. World War II and the socio-political climate in Japan before and during the war were no doubt factors in its apparent disappearance from the language teaching arena for a time. Palmer left Japan in 1936 (Henrichsen, 1989: 123-124). In 1955 the book was reissued in Tokyo, and a slightly revised edition of the same book was published in London in 1959. All editions are now out of print.

Palmer stated, "In view of the fact that the talking activities [of small children] are invariably preceded by a more or less long period of purely receptive work, mostly in the form of reacting physically to verbal stimuli, it would seem to be no exaggeration to state that the executing of orders is a prerequisite to the acquiring of powers of expression. I will therefore go so far as to suggest that no method of teaching foreign speech is likely to be economical or successful which does not include in the first period a very considerable proportion of that type of classroom work which consists in the carrying out by the pupil or pupils of orders issued by the teacher. Numerous experiments carried out in various countries under classroom conditions have shown with what extraordinary facility pupils become proficient in understanding and in executing orders" (1925: 43 and 1959: 39). He probably wrote this in 1924, since the "general introduction," which bears his name, is dated October, 1924.

In 1960, without knowing of Palmer's work, James J. Asher, Professor of Psychology at San José State University, undertook experiments to solve the conundrum of how to facilitate the acquisition of a second language. Early in his experimentation he hit upon the strategy of giving commands, modeling the physical responses to them and then having learners respond physically to them. Some of the results were immediately and clearly outstanding. This discovery led Asher to delve into why "the total physical response" achieved the extraordinary results that he observed. What was most notable was markedly superior comprehension of the spoken language. From that point on he has devoted a large part of his distinguished career to research on this question and to speaking and writing about it.

After publishing numerous articles on TPR in a variety of academic journals, in 1977 Asher published the first edition of *Learning Another Language Through Actions: The Complete Teacher's Guidebook*. When he began his investigations the language teaching environment was rather stagnant. Hardly anyone seemed to be looking for a better way. Professor Asher, however, knew that he was onto something exceptional. He began to carry out pedagogical research in an area in which little research had been done. He was, in fact, a pioneer not only in TPR but also in the broader field of language pedagogy. And he relentlessly pressed forward to get the word out that TPR brought results far beyond the usual.

About 15 years after Asher began his work on TPR, the language teaching environment began to flower — first in English as a Second Language, later in other languages. Now, 35 years after he did his first work on TPR, both Asher and his approach are widely known around the world. Asher's efforts have paid off.

While doing research to document the effectiveness of TPR, Asher continuously sought, by means of his deep and thorough knowledge of the field of experimental psychology, to explain *why* it is effective. In the second edition of *Learning Another Language Through Actions* (1982), Asher explained the role of the right hemisphere of the brain in "nature's design" for first language acquisition and how TPR relates to this design. In the third edition (1986) he undertook the unorthodox project — a right brain leap? — of writing a personal history of the development of TPR. In the fourth edition (1993) there were two major additions. One was the exposition of effective means of students' proceeding from facile comprehension of a quantity of the target language to oral production. Blaine Ray has made the major contribution in this significant advance in the realm of Total Physical Response through his work in teaching Spanish and ESL through what he calls "TPR Storytelling." The other major innovation in the fourth edition was the proposal that "brainswitching" is a major solution to the problem of "adaptation" in TPR. Adaptation in TPR is ceasing to respond (or responding grudgingly) to commands after having done so with gusto for a while. Brainswitching is engaging alternately in activities that make use of the right brain and the left brain.

Professor Asher has not stood still after discovering the magic of TPR. He has done varied research and he has spread the word widely. He has made a variety of TPR teaching and learning materials available through Sky Oaks Productions in Los Gatos, California. His work has made language teaching and study far more alive and effective for many thousands of language teachers and hundreds of thousands, probably millions, of language students. He has created an atmosphere that has allowed TPR to grow and flourish in unforeseeable ways. This flourishing has produced the seeds of further understanding on the part of Asher and the language teaching community. No doubt it will continue. TPR keeps evolving. Movement prevents stagnation.

Acknowledgments

We wish to give our heartfelt thanks to each of the following people, who graciously gave us assistance to make this book far better than it would otherwise be:

James J. Asher gave his encouragement in this project and his assistance with certain facts and opinions and contributed years of support.

Zev bar-Lev provided invaluable insights into fluency and connected discourse (p. 38).

Valerie and *Malcolm Benson* furnished invaluable information on the life and work of Harold Palmer (pp. *vii-viii*).

Andrew Blasky and *Elizabeth Chafcouloff* were helpful in the editing of the article which served as the basis for this book. It bore the same name as the book, was written by Contee Seely, and was published in the Japanese journal *Cross Currents* in the fall of 1982.

Berty Segal Cook has contributed various details, particularly her four levels of questioning (pp. 119-120) and her procedures for action series (pp. 25-26).

Rhoda Curtis has given continual support down through the years.

Jamie B. Draper of the American Council on the Teaching of Foreign Languages (ACTFL) furnished data on enrollment in foreign language courses in public high schools (p. 85).

James J. Duran helped with many years of instructive discussion and with specifics in regard to making the transition from a request form to present tense forms (pp. 89-91).

Carol Gaab gave us advice on using TPR Storytelling in ESL classes (p. 84).

Mary Galvan, Nick Kremer and *Roberta MacFarlane* provided significant information about research on the use of commands in various jobs (p. 11).

Leslie Harrison gave years of kindly moral support.

Cherie Hearne kindly drew the fine illustration on page 47.

Talmadge Heath has helped us in many ways.

Lynn Henrichsen provided useful facts on the work and career of Harold Palmer (pp. *vii-viii*).

Sally Sieloff Magnan of the *Modern Language Journal* helped with references on the percentage of students who continue to study languages in secondary schools (p. 85).

Frank McNulty verified the correctness of some French examples.

Joe Neilson offered salient ideas on details of TPR Storytelling (pp. 46, 47 and 58-62).

Lino Nivolo verified the accuracy of the analysis on page 90 for making the transition from imperative forms to the present tense in Italian.

Mary Sisk Noguchi gave encouragement and innovative ideas on using natural action dialogs in Japanese (pp. 111-113).

Jean-Paul Raffinot helped by verifying some of the French examples.

Blaine Ray provided much detailed information about his ever-improving brainchild, TPR Storytelling (Chapter 4, pp. 39-88) and much encouragement.

Maggie Seely put up with a lot and cared a lot.

Larry Statan for the use of his laser printer.

Christopher Taleck allowed us to use his lively drawings on pp. 55 and 68.

Robert Wachman gave years of encouragement and kindly pointed out errors in the first printing.

Chapter One:
Essential Questions About TPR

If you strip away all but the bare essentials of TPR, you end up with *a speech act which is related to a movement*. These two acts together form a wonderfully powerful language acquisition technique. Many thousands of language teachers have used it. They have used it in a tremendous diversity of circumstances. Some believe in the "direct method," allowing no language to be used other than the target language. Others do not believe this is necessary. Some have used this technique only in the form of a command followed by physical response. Others have included other combinations of speech act and movement. Some use it only very early in language training. Others use it even in advanced stages. Some do not require their students to talk until they spontaneously begin to talk. Others have them talk right away. And yet, despite all of these diverse ways of believing and teaching with *speech act-plus-movement*, virtually every teacher who has tried it has found it to be a wonderfully powerful language acquisition technique.

This book is about many of the ways this *speech act-plus-movement language acquisition technique* is effectively used. There is no way it can be all-inclusive, and we have no desire to make it so (although we are always pleased to hear about new effective ideas). In places this book contains contradictory advice. The technique itself is so powerful that — whatever else may be done along with it, whatever the teacher who is using it believes or

1

does — it is extremely effective. This is not to say that some ways of using it are not more productive than others, or more efficient, or less stressful, or...or...or... This book will show you many options. It is a part of the ever-growing extensive body of work that employs TPR and/or deals with it — a body of work which divulges many more options (see the references and bibliography on pp. 168-177).

Sometimes we strongly express opinions which are divergent in the extreme. No doubt you will use your own judgment. In the end what is decisive is not what anyone thinks is best but what works most effectively and efficiently for our students in their particular situations — what best helps them to acquire language — and, parenthetically, encourages them to do so with pleasure.

What Is TPR?

There are two common myths about James Asher's Total Physical Response (TPR):

1. that it consists of the use and performance of commands in the second or foreign language classroom — nothing more

2. that it is a method which is useful at the beginning level — not beyond

Let's have a look at Asher's own summary of TPR:

- Understanding the spoken language should be developed in advance of speaking.

- Understanding should be developed through movements of the student's body. The imperative is a powerful aid because the instructor can utter commands to manipulate student behavior. Our research suggests that most of the grammatical structure of the target language and hundreds of vocabulary items can be learned through the skillful use of the imperative by the instructor.

- Do not attempt to force speaking from students. As the students internalize a cognitive map of the target language through understanding what is heard, there will be a point of readiness to speak. The individual will spontaneously begin to produce utterances.

Asher, 1996: page 2-4

Clearly he emphasizes the imperative. However, his leading statement on movements is much broader: "Understanding should be developed through movements of the student's body." This allows for non-imperative ways of developing understanding of the spoken language through body movements.

The instructional strategy Asher proposes is based on an analysis of how children acquire their first language (Asher, 1972: 133-139; 1996: pages 2-3 and 2-4). Obviously children move their bodies in response to language other than commands. Many non-imperative statements — "Can I play with your doll?" "Do you want a cookie?" "This ball is mine." — are very likely to produce a physical response in a small child who is developing an understanding of the spoken language. Asher relates Piaget's work (see Piaget, 1955) to recent evidence on the functioning of the hemispheres of the brain:

> The infant begins to decode sights and sounds by looking, grasping, touching, pulling, pushing, sucking — all non-verbal motor movement. The infant in the sensorimotor months is tracing a map of how things work, including language. This mapping in the right hemisphere through direct manipulation is necessary for the more advanced construction of concepts in the left hemisphere that result in talking, thinking in logical, linear patterns, and solving problems through symbols — words, numbers, and internalized concepts.
>
> Asher, 1981: 63

We therefore consider that TPR is in play in any situation in which the target language is used meaningfully with movement. With this broader than usual concept of TPR, it is possible to accomplish much more than with commands alone. This book is also about ancillary activities, activities that are based on TPR having been used before they take place.

What Can Be Accomplished with TPR?
What Can It Not Do?

What are its strengths? What are its weaknesses? One of its greatest strengths, from any point of view, is that it develops listening comprehension efficiently and pleasantly. There is carryover to other skills, particularly reading comprehension if the first language of the student and the target language share a common alphabet. Among the "four skills," the productive skills of speaking and writing are the weaker. However, as you will see in Chapters 3 ("Fluency & Connected Discourse") and 4 ("TPR Storytelling"), nearly any student can achieve fluency by using TPR as the basis for language acquisition.

Many, if not most, teachers who have used it for vocabulary development find that it is superior to other ways of developing vocabulary, at least when used for concrete vocabulary, such as action verbs, names of objects, prepositions of place and many adjectives and adverbs — any vocabulary which can be easily demonstrated by physical means. For the internalization of less obvious vocabulary items, it can also be extremely effective. See especially the following sections regarding vocabulary: "Steps for Acquiring New Vocabulary" (pp. 8-10), pp. 17-18 in "Action Series," and pp. 44-56 in "Learning to Tell a Story — Step by Step."

Why TPR Is Effective

Asher believes that nature's model of first language acquisition "continues to operate when an individual — child or adult — attempts to learn a second or third language" (1996: page 2-24) and that TPR fits the model more closely than other contemporary approaches (1981: 63-66). He feels that TPR especially "is in harmony with the biological program" (1996: page 2-4), because it uses body movement extensively both before and after speech appears and because it does not require the learner to speak before s/he is ready to speak. Recent discoveries about the workings of the right and left hemispheres of the brain support Asher's findings:

> The right and left hemispheres of the brain process information independently.... The left brain seems to communi-

cate through speech while the right brain is mute, but can communicate through physical behavior such as pointing, touching, drawing, singing, gesturing, and pantomime. TPR instruction may permit the student to process information through the right brain while traditional formats such as the audio-lingual or translation approaches may be oriented almost exclusively to left brain processing.

Asher, 1996: page 3-18

This "harmony with the biological program" accounts in large part for the "minimum of stress" (1996: page 2-4) in TPR, another reason for its effectiveness. There is evidence from learning and memory research that high anxiety or stress in a learning situation brings about poorer learning than low anxiety or none (Loftus, 1980: 82). In investigating the acquisition of language specifically, Krashen finds that *"low* anxiety relates [positively] to success in second language acquisition" (1981: 56).

> WARNING: Stress *can* occur with TPR if it is misused —
> for example, if the teacher is angry, negative or overly
> authoritarian. If a teacher has any tendency to get
> stressed, s/he is advised to be aware of this and take
> whatever measures possible to relax and be positive.

A further reason for TPR's effectiveness is its believability. Asher postulates that an utterance which refers to a factual, primary experience of the learner is more believable than an utterance which refers to something not experienced live and directly (1996: page 3-17). In a discussion of first language learning, Asher mentions three basic principles of learning that relate to believability in particular and which are regularly used in TPR. They are three more ways that TPR approximates what occurs in first language learning:

The first principle ... is *contiguity.* The ... word "Run!," for example, immediately precedes the action in oneself and others.... The second principle is *frequency* of pairing between the symbol ... and the referent.... And the third principle is *feedback.* When the ... utterance appears, the predicted action always follows. There is a cause-effect relationship which validates the connection as truth.

1981: 60

Finally, Asher puts forth a motor skills hypothesis. He contends that TPR causes "keen activation of the kinesthetic sensory system or 'muscle learning'" (1996: 3-17) which brings about long-term recall as in manual skills.

To this motor skills hypothesis, let us add its complement, the emotional involvement hypothesis, according to which there is keen activation of the *emotional* system. TPR enlivens a class by creating stimulating experiences, so that students are in a more lively state and the learning thus has a strong emotional base, as well as a physical base. Research indicates that "highly newsworthy events ... and personally significant events can leave one with what is called a flashbulb memory." The explanation given for such long-term recall of "flashbulb" memories is this: "The main ingredient seems to be a very high level of surprise, often accompanied by emotional arousal" (Loftus, 1980: 126-127).

Emotional arousal can increase anxiety. And yet we have said that a *low* level of anxiety is most conducive to effective language learning. So, we should qualify the emotional involvement hypothesis by saying that levels and kinds of emotional arousal must be controlled so that the level of anxiety of the learner remains "low." The instructor should always try to be aware of the level of anxiety the learners are experiencing and should be ready to take steps to change the level and kind of emotional arousal. When there is pleasant emotional arousal, students pay close attention. They become lively and receptive and even reach out to receive. There is no chance of dozing off or of boredom.

We have dealt with several reasons for the effectiveness of TPR. Here is a brief summary of them:

1. Close approximation to nature's design for language learning as described by Piaget.
2. Right brain hypothesis.
3. Minimal stress and anxiety.
4. Believability hypothesis (and the contiguity, frequency and feedback principles).
5. Motor skills hypothesis.
6. Emotional involvement hypothesis.

Explaining TPR to Your Class

When a class first begins to use TPR exercises, sometimes there is resistance to them. Students may have never experienced anything like TPR in a class before. They may feel that it is unnecessary to actually do things or that it is childish. It is useful to explain to a class, perhaps especially a class which is not starting from scratch with TPR, how it will be more effective and rewarding than other approaches to language learning. The most obvious factors are:

- It makes a great difference in listening comprehension (understanding the spoken word).
- If you can already understand something before you say it, it will be easier to say it.
- There's real or realistic communication happening all the time.
- It's fun and active and involving.

Among the reasons mentioned above on pp. 4-6 for its effectiveness you may want to mention especially the close approximation to nature's design for language learning (how we learn our first language) and the believability hypothesis. You may want to mention and emphasize different things to students of different ages. To children under the age of puberty there is probably no need to say anything, though you may wish to say something like, "We're going to have fun. We're going to learn Spanish (English, French, Japanese, German, Italian, Russian, Chinese...)."

When to Use TPR, When Not To

TPR is chiefly an aural-oral approach, so it is not *directly* useful for the learning of reading or writing, except for certain limited exercises aimed primarily at low-level students (such commands like "Write your name," "Write these letters: m-o-m," "Point to the word *apple*" and "Run to the sentence *I love you* and kiss it."). Of course, a variety of reading and writing activities can be based on content used in aural and aural-oral TPR activities, and reading and writing would certainly reinforce material internalized through TPR. (For a number of ideas about writing activities, see Chapter 7, pp. 139-153.)

DEFINITION: *Internalize* in TPR means that a student becomes so familiar with a term that s/he can instantly respond to it physically upon hearing it. In many cases it also indicates that a student has reached the point where s/he is able to produce the term easily.

Any piece of language can be acquired through TPR. Objects, maps and illustrations can be very useful in demonstrating and practicing. Any concept that cannot be demonstrated actively should be presented some other way. Some bits of language can be demonstrated live only with difficulty or with ambiguity. If you can't do it without tremendous difficulty or without ambiguity, one option is to clarify by translating. (See "Ways and Means of Getting Across Meaning" on pp. 26-28.) Usually you can give a translation very quickly and then immediately return to the target language. *The acquisition has only just begun with the clarification of meaning.* Once the meaning is clear, you can get on with the process of internalizing the vocabulary item through the aural input of TPR commands and descriptions.

Steps for Acquiring New Vocabulary

TPR is a very, very good way to teach vocabulary. The various steps involved in the acquisition of a new term through TPR are:

- The presentation of meaning (see "Ways and Means of Getting Across Meaning" on pp. 26-28)
- Internalization
- Early production
- Semi-fluent production in various contexts
- Fluent production in many contexts

Above we observed that in some instances it is necessary or preferable to present a new term through means other than TPR. It is worth noting, too, that TPR is not always the best or the only approach for the other steps. It is wise to use several ways to provide comprehensible input; they will certainly assist in internalization and they provide variety, which is extremely important. For working towards greater fluency, action dialogs and action role-playing are only two of many useful tools that can provide excellent production practice.

It would seem that abstractions such as *justice, government, prospect* and *biology* could not be actively demonstrated with clarity and ease. However, if such terms are placed into context, there is a way to demonstrate them actively.

Blaine Ray, the originator of TPR Storytelling, tells mini-stories to demonstrate many abstractions in a meaningful context. For example, to demonstrate *justice*, he uses a mini-story like the following:

> John steals a thousand dollars. A policeman catches him.
> He goes to court. The judge throws him in jail. Justice: if
> you steal, you go to jail.

The story is acted out by students for clarity and impact. Everything in it is demonstrable. By retelling it a number of times as it is being reperformed by students, the word *justice* is internalized by the class. For more on mini-stories in TPR Storytelling, see pp. 42-43 and 51-54.

Once its meaning is made clear, by whatever means, any word can be internalized through TPR. (See the discussion of abstractions and idioms in Asher, 1996: pages 3-20 through 3-22.) One option mentioned by Asher is to write such words on cards and manipulate them like concrete objects. However, this certainly is not live, direct, primary, factual experience in the sense used above. In any event it is possible to delay the learning of an abstraction until learners comprehend sufficient concrete vocabulary to understand an explanation of it and/or to infer its meaning from context.

Following are a couple of examples of the internalization of abstractions after the meaning has been presented through means other than TPR:

- Illustrations of a few animals can be given to students on paper, and they can be told: "Study biology;" they carry out the command by examining the animals.

(They can also be instructed to draw them themselves before studying them.)

• A capital building can be drawn on the board, and students can tell one another such things as:

"Go to the government."

"Throw tomatoes at the government."

"Ignore the government."

Additionally, natural action dialogs (see pp. 28-32) and action role plays (see pp. 32-33) can be created by students or the teacher to practice an abstraction after its meaning has been established.

Terms such as *while* and *a long way* are sometimes considered abstractions, but these can be directly demonstrated. For instance, see the following exercises: number 5 on page 14 and the example on page 136. We suggest you read what Asher has to say about acquiring abstractions and idioms on pages 3-20 through 3-22 in *Learning Another Language Through Actions*.

For more on teaching vocabulary, see pp. 17-19 in the next chapter and pp. 44-56 in Chapter 4.

Using TPR in Conjunction with a Given Curriculum, Book or Syllabus

Asher has shown that the results in terms of students' achievement in listening comprehension, speaking, reading and writing are likely to be superior if TPR is used (Asher, 1996: page 2-5 to page 2-17). In terms of retention, minimized stress, emotional involvement, ease of interaction, confidence, full experience and motivation, the results are also likely to be superior. Much of the vocabulary can be presented through TPR (see "Ways and Means of Getting Across Meaning" on pp. 26-28), and all the vocabulary, including vocabulary that has not been presented through TPR, can be practiced and internalized through TPR and "hand TPR" — the use of gestures or hand signals to represent vocabulary items (see pp. 41 and 44-49). The same advantages pertain when the goal of a course is to prepare students to pass a certain exam, even if the skills to be tested are reading and writing, including translation.

Using TPR in Vocational ESL

There is a special advantage to sequences of imperatives for ESL students who have jobs or expect to get them soon. Commands are used with great frequency in most, if not all, job areas. A research project done in Texas in 1979-80 by the Resource Development Institute of Austin, under the direction of Mary Galvan, showed that in over 4,000 oral samples of language on the job a full 40% involved imperatives! The samples were gathered from 12 diverse fields of work, including business, welding, health, food service and auto mechanics. The same study also indicated that most verbs are useful in all vocations, whereas nouns tend to be specific to a particular occupation. These findings strongly suggest that responding to and producing series of commands are highly useful to students involved in a variety of endeavors.

Chapter 2:
Four Basic Types of TPR Exercises

In this chapter we present four basic types of TPR exercises. There are various subtypes. And there are innumerable types of exercises which can supplement them. We won't discuss any of these here but refer you to the valuable presentations of techniques throughout *Instructor's Notebook: How to Apply TPR for Best Results* (García, 1988) and in Chapter 2 of *Fluency Through TPR Storytelling* (Ray and Seely, 1998). Here we will deal with:

1. *Single Commands and Descriptions,* unrelated commands and combining exercises.
2. *Action Series,* also known as action sequences, action-logues, action chains, operations, cycles or audio-motor units.
3. *Natural Action Dialogs,* including role-playing dialogs and skits.
4. *Action Role-Playing* without a prepared script.

Only the first two types are "classical TPR." The other two may derive from these or from other sources. If the two classical types are used before the others or along with them so that students have thoroughly internalized the relevant vocabulary, the latter two are likely to be more lively and more effective. In addition to the examples given in this chapter, there are numerous others throughout the book.

Single Commands and Descriptions

Unrelated Commands and Descriptions

1. Erect an edifice.
2. Grapple with your opponent.
3. Search for the torch that Hiro mislaid.
4. If you have some matches, please lend them to me.
5. They were sleeping while we were eating.
6. Martina is eating marshmallows.
7. The building collapsed.
8. It's going to rain.
9. She had left when I got there.

In the first two examples, the emphasis is on vocabulary. The first three are commands; the last six are descriptions. They involve actions which can be acted out or simulated or pantomimed in class. In the last six, the emphasis is on structure, with the assumption that the vocabulary is already quite familiar to the students—most likely having been introduced through commands.

TIP: You might wonder about how to introduce the verb *rain* with a command. Do two things — establish a context and use "hand TPR" (see pp. 41 and 44-49):

It's raining. Open your umbrella.

Both the raining and the opening of the umbrella can be simulated by using hand motions.

It is essential that students be very familiar with the vocabulary that they meet in new structures they are acquiring.

Combining Exercises

1.

		nose.
Caress		patella.
	your	scapula.
Wiggle		gastrocnemius.
		sternocleidomastoid.

2.

Please	hammer	like crazy.
	laugh	innocently.
Don't	flutter your eyes	lightly.

Combining exercises can be a step along the road to fluent free speech, allowing practice in creating sentences of one structure at a time while selecting words from a limited repertoire. Such exercises, also called substitution tables, originated no later than 1524 when one by Erasmus appeared (Kelly, 1969: 101). They can be used on the board, on an overhead projector or on paper. They work well for production as long as the number of elements being used is kept down to a manageable number, according to the level of the group. The number of elements can be increased in a given exercise after a class has begun to work with it. Students can suggest elements to make up the original exercise or to add on.

After producing several sentences from such a table, the logical next step for students is to create some more sentences with the same structure *without referring to a table*. If necessary for some learners, a single sentence might remain in view as a sample. Generally, if the level of the structure is appropriate for the students, this is not necessary.

The above examples are all of simple command sentences, but of course all sorts of other sentences can be worked on with combining exercises, all of which can involve action. Take, for instance, sentence number 9 from the list above, on page 14, a somewhat complex sentence involving both the simple past and the past perfect:

She		left		I		got	there.
The train		arrived		George		woke up	in Maine
	had		when				
Wanda						finished	at the board
		eaten		the 49ers			

15

Numerous combinations are possible with the elements of this table, which contains 21 words. All the combinations can be acted out.

Here's an example of how to handle this combining exercise:

1. A train could be drawn on the board, though this is probably not necessary. (The quality of the drawing would make no difference.) A rough map of Maine can be scribbled on the board. Anyone can take the part of Wanda or George, or students' names can be substituted for them.

2. The teacher and a student or two — or two or three students — choose a combination among themselves, without telling the rest of their group or the rest of the class, for example: *The train had left when the 49ers woke up at the board.*

3. While the rest of the group or class watches, they act out the sentence. Since these combinations all form sentences that occur entirely in the past, the action precedes the saying of the sentence. One person acts like the train. Two others act like the 49ers.

4. After the rest of the group has seen the actions occur, someone among them describes it, producing the sentence, "The train had left when the 49ers woke up at the board."

This particular example is rather complex. In some cases, only one actor or actress will suffice.

TIP: For sentences involving the first person (*I, we, me, us*) or the second person (*you*, singular or plural), hand signals can be used before the action occurs (see pp. 114-115). You will want to be sure they are culturally appropriate.

Action Series

These are also known as action sequences, action chains, actionlogues, operations, audiomotor units (this term, referring to action series created for the purpose of teaching cultural detail, was introduced in Kalivoda, Morain and Elkins, 1971) and cycles. Such series, perhaps without action, go back at least as far as Pseudo-Dositheus in 250 A.D. (Kelly, 1969: 115). They were later developed more fully by Gouin (1880). Harold E. Palmer and his daughter Dorothée (1925) were perhaps the first to use them with action.

Command Action Series

1. Pick up the bottle of vitamin pills.
   Take the top off.
   Take out a pill.
   Take the pill.
   > adapted from Romijn and Seely, 1988: 8

2. Strip the label off of the plastic bottle.
   Crush it with your hands.
   Throw it on the ground.
   Stomp on it continually until it is as flat as possible.
   Lean over and pick it up.
   Finally, deposit it in the recycling container.

Both series emphasize vocabulary. The first example is a kind of series called an operation — a normal sequence of actions used to accomplish an ordinary procedure. Other examples are sharpening a pencil and using a pay phone. (This term is used with this specific meaning by Gayle Nelson and Thomas Winters in their 1980 book *ESL Operations*; the revised, expanded edition (1993) is called *Operations in English*; see pp. 23-24 and 174.)

3. You've got to wash your grubby, filthy hands.
   Grasp the faucet.
   Struggle to turn it on.
   Pick up the soap with your left hand from the soap dish.
   Scrub your hands for 20 to 30 seconds while you count.
   Rinse your hands off slowly and thoroughly.
   Don't forget to clean under your fingernails.
   > adapted from Romijn and Seely, 1988: 1

(The original version of this series is given below.) These three command action series, as they stand above, are obviously of different levels. It is always possible to adapt an action series to a different level (or for different purposes). This is mainly a matter of adding or subtracting detail. Some entire lines may be added or deleted. Or just words or phrases. Sentence structure in many cases can be made more complicated or, sometimes, simpler. In the third series above there is a lot of structure and a lot of vocabulary, most of which is clarified in the first demonstrations of the series. Until vocabulary becomes *internalized* or very familiar, students do not attempt to use these structures in real oral give and take. A command action series with such complex content as this one would not be used with beginners. For intermediate students, it might be strictly a listening comprehension exercise which would lead to internalizaton of the more sophisticated portions of it. If you wanted intermediate or advanced students to produce this sequence, you would work on any structural feature that had not been mastered by members of the class before expecting production. See the sections below on teaching structure through "Natural Action Dialogs" (pp. 91-113 and 123-136).

WASHING YOUR HANDS

1. You're going to wash your hands.

2. Turn on the water.

3. Pick up the soap.

4. Wash your hands.

5. Put the soap down.

6. Rinse your hands.

7. Turn off the water.

8. Pick up the towel.

9. Dry your hands.

10. Put the towel on the towel rack.

Romijn and Seely, 1988: 1

18

An action series can be considered a vocabulary lesson on which to base lessons on practically any grammar point you wish to emphasize. Once students have mastered the vocabulary of an action series, there are numerous possible ways to put it to use to build more skills and acquire more language. See "Natural Action Dialogs" on pp. 28-32 and also Chapter 5, "Acquiring Tenses through TPR," and Chapter 6, "Acquiring Other Grammatical Features and Idioms and Expressions with TPR."

Minidrama

One variation of action series is what Dale Griffee calls a "minidrama." What distinguishes it from other series is that there are always two or more actors or physical respondents to whom the reader or director addresses the commands. When any exchange of dialog between actors is included, this is accomplished through "directed dialog," the reader telling the actors what to say.

"Cops and Robbers"
1. This is a street.
2. You are a robber. Put on a mask.
3. You are a man. Walk down the street.
4. Robber, tell the man, "Stop!"
5. Tell the man, "Put up your hands and give me your money."
6. Man, give the robber your money.
7. Robber, take the money and run.
8. You are a policeman. This is a police car.
9. Open the door, get into the police car and drive the police car.
10. Man, look for a policeman.
11. Yell, "Police, police!"
12. Policeman, stop the police car and get out.
13. Ask the man, "What's the matter?"
14. Man, tell the policeman, "A robber took my money."
15. Policeman, ask the man, "Where is the robber?"
16. Man, tell the policeman, "I don't know."
17. Policeman, tell the man, "Get into the car."
18. Man, get into the police car.

19. Look for the robber.
20. You see the robber. Point to the robber.
21. Tell the policeman, "That's the man. He took my money."
22. Policeman, stop the car, open the door, get out of the police car and run to the robber. Take the robber to the police car.
23. Man, get out of the police car.
24. Tell the policeman, "Thank you."
25. Policeman, put the robber in the police car. Drive to the police station.

> Adapted from Griffee, 1981: 47; with additional material from the original manuscript

"Iffy" or Conditional Series

If you have on a blue or checkered shirt, wave to me.
If you have on a shirt of another color or pattern, stand up.
If you don't have on a shirt but have on something else instead, sigh.

The "iffy" series is not a series in the usual sense, though it is a connected group of commands. Students can acquire a lot of vocabulary through iffy series used as comprehension exercises.

Procedures for Single Commands and Descriptions and for Action Series

The purpose of these procedures is to prepare the students to work in pairs or in small groups, speaking and doing actions. The procedures may be varied — some omitted, some repeated — according to what needs to be done to adequately prepare students to work on their own. The following procedures are based largely on procedures in Romijn and Seely (1988: ix-xv) and in part on procedures in Segal (1992: 2). Other sets of procedures are provided afterwards, two sets from other prominent action series textbooks and one which is used by Berty Segal Cook (a.k.a. Berty Segal). Note that the following procedures are useful with action series as well as with single commands and descriptions. Examples of action series are on pp. 18 and 22.

A. Listening (Receptive Stage)

1. Setting Up: Introducing and reminding of names of objects and places. Objects (even plastic or rubber facsimiles), maps and illustrations (even if crude) are often very helpful in demonstrating and practicing.

2. Initial Demonstration: Giving of commands/descriptions by the instructor, followed by appropriate actions by the instructor and/or students.

3. Group Live Action: Students do the actions at the appropriate time in relation to statements made by the instructor without the instructor modeling any of the actions. When the group shows it is ready to speak by unhesitating response to commands (or in some other way), proceed to the next stage.

B. Speaking (Expressive Stage)

4. Repeat the above listening steps as necessary (if done in the next class session).

5. Oral Repetition of Commands or Descriptions: Students may follow the words or the cue pictures on the board or the overhead projector screen or on paper. This step helps students to get things right and pronounce with confidence. In some circumstances it is unnecessary. Ask the students. If some feel it is useful, it probably is.

6. Speaking and Live Action: Individual students speak and do actions at appropriate times while the group observes. The speaker and the doers are different people, unless the speaking is in the first person (*I* or *we*). The students may be volunteers or may be selected by the teacher. The teacher may participate in doing actions.

7. Oral repetition again (when useful).

8. Pair Work: Students working in pairs, speaking and doing actions at appropriate times, all working at the same time. This step is often noisy and chaotic. It is

helpful to use a bell or horn or other signal to call the class to order when the time comes. With certain groups of children, this can get out of hand. If you can't get it to work this way, you can have them do the action one pair at a time.

9. Written Reinforcement: The students may copy the material, if desired, or you may dictate it to them. (See "TPR Dictation," pp. 139-141.) This may be done just before or after Step 5 above, if preferred. Another way to do this for action series and dialogs is to write out the format of the material with or without a few cue words. For example:

Pick ____ ____ ___ _____ vitamin _____ .

_____ off _____ _____ .

_____ out ____ _____ .

_____ _____ pill.

(The complete version of this series is given below.)

VITAMIN PILL

1. You're going to take your vitamins

2. Pick up the bottle of vitamin pills.

3. Take the top off.

4. Take out a pill.

5. Put the top back on.

6. Put the bottle down.

7. Put the pill in your mouth.

8. Drink some water and swallow the pill.

9. Uh-oh! It's stuck in your throat!

10. Drink some more water.

11. O.K. Good. It went down.

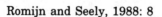

Romijn and Seely, 1988: 8

The above procedures are essentially those presented in *Live Action English* (Romijn and Seely: 1988). Since the first edition of *Live Action English* appeared in 1979, numerous different ways of using the action series in the book have come to our attention. There are also other books of action series (see pp. 174-175 for a full listing), and the authors of them present different ideas about how to use action series. Below we present the basic procedures suggested in two of these, *Actionlogues* by Joanne "Jody" Klopp (1985) and *Operations in English* by Gayle Nelson and Thomas Winters (1993) as well as those used by Berty Segal Cook (a.k.a. Berty Segal).

Actionlogues contains a photograph for each line in every action series. There are 25 units and 160 lines and photos. Rather than presenting a whole action series in order from the beginning, Klopp takes a basically different tack. After she has presented 3 or 4 commands, she starts mixing them up or "recombining" them, as is done in "classical" TPR. Each verb is used with a variety of nouns, etc., as she continues the practice. She gradually adds in more and more commands from the action series, all the while recombining and practicing, until the whole series is presented. She also commands students to do what she calls "mini-actionlogues," shortened action series. She consciously avoids going through a series the same way each time "to eliminate sequence memorization" (p. *ii*). These are the procedures for listening comprehension.

She allows speaking to emerge whenever students "show a readiness" — in a week or several months (p. *iv*), although she does recommend "reading aloud," in which the students repeat after the teacher and then give commands to one another in groups. During this activity some original commands are created by students, apparently without urging.

Operations in English by Gayle Nelson and Thomas Winters (1993) consists of 55 operations — mostly succinct procedures for doing ordinary activities of modern life, such as using a cassette recorder, following simple recipes, mailing a letter, using a self-serve gasoline pump, etc. Nelson and Winters suggest the following ways of using their operations:

1. The teacher introduces the materials and new vocabulary, naming objects and their parts.
2. The teacher gives the directions and performs the actions.
3. The students open their books.
4. Optional: choral repetition.
5. Two students model the operation.
6. Pair practice by all students.
7. Practice with books closed.   (pp. 3-4)

A 2nd way:

1. Students read the operation.
2. Students ask the teacher questions on pronunciation, vocabulary, grammar, comprehension.
3. Two students or the teacher and one student perform the operation, one speaking, the other performing.
4. Pair practice by all students.
5. Practice with books closed.   (p. 5)

A 3rd way (pp. 5-6), used after students are used to working in pairs, gives the students the opportunity to figure out the operation. The teacher must be careful that the selected operation is one that the students can do on their own. S/he must make sure they have whatever materials are necessary.

1. Student A, whose book is open, reads the operation to Student B, whose book is closed. Student B performs the actions.
2. Same as Step 1 with roles reversed.
3. Same as Step 1, with both books closed.
4. Same as Step 2, with both books closed.

One of the authors' many useful suggestions is to have students attach appropriate transitional and softening phrases or words to the commands, namely: *first, next, now, next you, please, would you please, at this point you should, now try to, next you can, finally you're ready to, you will (can, may, should)* _____ *now, would you mind; OK, now.* (p. 8)

Another set of fruitful procedures is recommended for elementary and secondary school classes by noted TPR author and teacher trainer Berty Segal Cook (a.k.a. Berty Segal):

1. The teacher reads the series aloud line by line as s/he acts it out along with 2 or 3 students.
2. S/he reads it again and models it again, this time as the entire class acts it out along with her/him.
3. The class reads the entire series in chorus. This step may follow Step 6 instead or may be repeated after Step 6.
4. Every student is given a rubber band or a clip and a large sheet of paper, at least 11" by 17" (28 x 43 cm.), preferably 18" by 24" (45 x 61 cm.) or even larger. Lined paper is best for this exercise.
5. One of the following is done:
    a. Secondary school. The teacher places before the class a large copy of the series which has been prepared beforehand. This large copy must be easily readable from every student's seat. It may be written on a reusable poster or on the chalkboard.
    b. Elementary school. Students are each given a book (sometimes one book for each two students to share) which contains the series; if books are not available, they are given a photocopy of the series on paper from which to write out their own copy.
6. Each student copies each line of the series in large writing onto her or his large sheet, numbering each line in order.
7. Working in pairs, one student reads each line of the series to her or his partner, pausing between lines for the partner to perform the action. Then the actor becomes the reader and vice versa.
8. Each student now draws a picture at the end of each line of the sequence to represent the action of the line. Generally speaking, the larger the paper, the easier and quicker it is for students to make these drawings. There is no need for the drawings to be fine. Each stu-

dent will use her or his own drawings a little later. When this is done, there are a number, a sentence and a drawing on each line.

9. The students cut their papers into strips, one line per strip, with number, sentence and drawing.

10. Each student mixes up her or his strips and then puts a rubber band or a clip on the whole set to hold it together.

11. Now each student puts the strips in order, or this may be done in pairs with one set of strips.

12. The students mix up their strips again. Then the teacher tells the students to fold the numbers back so that they cannot be seen. Again they put the strips in order, this time without the help of the numbers. (This may also be done in pairs.)

13. The students cut off the pictures with scissors and mix them up. They then put the pictures in the order of the series and clip or bind the set of pictures together. (This too may be done in pairs.)

14. Working in pairs, students read the text on their strips to each other in order, each one following and checking her or his partner's reading.

15. Still working in pairs, each student produces orally the whole series in order, using her or his own pictures as cues while the partner listens and checks.

16. On a regular-sized sheet of paper, each student individually writes out the entire series in order, using the pictures as cues.

Note that in this process students become thoroughly familiar with the series as they listen, read, copy, speak and write.

Ways and Means of Getting Across Meaning

The *criteria* here are:

1. Clarity

2. Efficiency — get the meaning across quickly and then get on with doing the other things that need to be done for students to acquire the vocabulary item. Don't spend any more time than absolutely necessary on getting meaning across.

(Blaine Ray says, "Time is our greatest enemy" in language teaching.)

Demonstration With Commands

Many actions are obvious, like *stand up*. Also many concrete nouns are obvious when an action is used with them, as in *drive the car*. Some adverbs are obvious when used with actions, as in *hit the table softly* and *clap softly*. Most prepositions of place are too, as in put the money between the glass and the plate. If the concept can be gotten across quickly through TPR, this is the best way.

TPR Demonstration Without Commands

Buy can be quickly demonstrated. The teacher tells a student to bring forward his/her pencil. Then s/he gives the student some money and takes the pencil while saying the single word "buy" or a sentence, "I *buy* the pencil" or "I'm *buy*ing the pencil."

Showing

The meaning of *clothing* is evident from just tugging on or touching various pieces of clothing. If there are not (1) real objects to show, the teacher can show (2) phony ones (rubber, plastic, toys, whatever) or (3) color or (4) black-and-white photos or (5) paintings or (6) drawings. TPR expert Berty Segal Cook (a.k.a. Berty Segal) believes the more real or realistic the object or illustration, the more effective the presentation of the vocabulary item (as reflected in the order given above). But the main point is to get the meaning across quickly and clearly and then carry on with other activities.

Translation

The teacher will often give a translation of a word quickly or have a student do so. The way the meaning is conveyed depends on the circumstances of the class. In a class in which all learners share a common language, like a French class in the United States, the teacher would probably just say "beautiful" immediately after saying "belle" or "beau." In a class of learners with several first languages, like many urban ESL classes in the U.S. and the U.K., a student from each language group could look up a word in a bilingual dictionary and tell the other speakers of the language the meaning.

Natural Action Dialogs

These are dialogs in which action is performed with or without commands. The word *dialog* is not being used here in exactly the sense that it is usually used in language classrooms, where it refers to a short script which is presented as a whole to students, then taught to them and finally spoken by them. The difference here is that instead of presenting a finished dialog, the dialog is *developed* in a *natural* give and take between the teacher and the students. Because there is *action* and real *context* present at all times, the students respond truthfully to questions about an immediate situation which has been put before them. Then the teacher's questions and the students' responses become the dialog to practice and learn. A number of examples of natural action dialogs are described thoroughly on pp. 91-113 in Chapter 5, "Acquiring Tenses," and on pp. 123-136 in Chapter 6, "Acquiring Other Grammatical Features and Idioms and Expressions."

The key here is the word *natural* as in Stephen Krashen and Tracy Terrell's Natural Approach (see Krashen and Terrell, 1983). The most essential idea in the Natural Approach is that language is *acquired* "by using it in natural, communicative situations," rather than being *learned* by having "a conscious knowledge about grammar" (p. 18). Krashen and Terrell say, "The core of the Natural Approach classroom is a series of *acquisition activities* [their emphasis]." Each activity "must be interesting or meaningful so that the students' attention is focused on the content of the utterances instead of the form" (p. 97). That is what we want to do here, the only addition being that in "natural action dialogs" there is always action.

There are many reasons to make the communication natural: to lower stress, to more closely approximate first language acquisition, to use the right brain, to make the lessons more fun and enjoyable. But what we would like to emphasize here is that striving to make the dialogs natural and the conversation real and immediate will cause you to create a context which will make clear the meaning not only of the vocabulary you're using but also of the grammatical structures you intend for the students to acquire. Clear context is essential so that the students can use what they already know to understand and then acquire and learn their new language.

Many language materials and lessons deal only with the *formulation* of a structure and meaning. Furthermore, many that do present something about use and meaning do not get beyond a *presentation or explanation* of it, so that when the lesson gets to the practice stage, only the *form* is drilled or practiced, but not the circumstances in which it is used, leaving the students with a structure which they may know how to formulate perfectly, but which they have only a very vague idea of when to use. The result is that they don't use it at all!

Even if the various circumstances in which a structure is used are explained and examples are given, students may understand them without having acquired a "feel" for when the circumstances are present to *use* the structure. For most students it is not enough to *understand* the circumstances. They must *experience* them.

This is the reason it is crucial to use natural action dialogs and to repeat them, varying the content while repeating the circumstances which require the use of the structure. The explanations and examples given by an instructor or a textbook provide the opportunity to *learn about* when to use a structure. The experiencing of circumstances in which it is used provide the opportunity both to *acquire* it and to *acquire a feel* for when to use it.

In some cases students need to see the whole situation in order to experience and understand the circumstances that are relevant to an appropriate use of a structure — which may mean that they need to see and hear it develop over time. For many languages, two things are often significant in determining what structure and what verb tense to use :

- The time when one action occurs in relation to another
- The time when an action occurs in relation to the time when a sentence is spoken

Of course, each particular structure has its own pertinent conditions for determining appropriate use.

The lessons in this section give practice in the formulation of the structure *simultaneously* with its use and its meaning in an obvious context. Therefore the students come away not only trained to say it correctly but feeling confident of at least some of the appropriate situations in which to use it.

One difference between the Natural Approach acquisition activities and natural action dialogs is that we believe it is useful to point out to students what situation a structure is used in. Being aware of this will help some students; it can't hurt. Still, we believe that the most important factor in acquiring a structure is the active experiencing of it *in context*, preferably in several examples of each appropriate context.

Besides structural or grammatical points, natural action dialogs may focus on idioms and other expressions.

Some of the examples given are dialogs based on action series which have been previously mastered by the learners. It is often possible and at times essential to do this. It is useful to think of an action series as a vocabulary lesson on which can be based lessons on practically any grammar point you wish to emphasize. Once students have mastered the vocabulary (see "Procedures for Single Commands and Descriptions and for Action Series" on pp. 20-26), you can *use* their new vocabulary to build more skills and acquire more language. If you want to include unfamiliar material in a natural action dialog, you must work on this beforehand through commands or other means that ensure internalization of it before you begin work on the natural action dialog. Action series are often very helpful in this regard, essential, in fact, in cases where the sequence of events is critical to the usage and meaning of a structure, e.g., whether a certain event occurs before or after another or has already happened or has yet to take place.

After selecting a grammatical feature or an idiom to help students to acquire, a teacher must go through certain steps to accomplish this end:

1. Determine at least one context or set of circumstances in which the structure or idiom is commonly used. This normally just means thinking of some examples of the use of the structure and then carefully examining the contexts in which they are used.

After settling on one context:

2. Formulate the questions that will elicit the desired appropriate responses from the students. For examples see pp. 91-113 and 123-136. The only new element in the resulting dialog should be the particular structure or idiom to be acquired. Students should be thoroughly familiar with everything else in the natural action dialog; they should have internalized and already be producing all the rest.

   On occasion there may be more than one element that is being worked on at one time. For example, in the "pantomime game" below, which is used to help students acquire the present continuous in English (or the simple present in some languages), a second point of structure that might be worked on simultaneously is the use of possessive adjectives as in the sentence *She's washing **her** hands*. This would be done only if the particular class had already begun to produce it in this context and/or if the teacher knows from experience that the group is capable enough to deal with it. In this instance the particular circumstance that determines that this is an appropriate use of the possessive adjective in English is that the reference is to a part of the body of the person being spoken about. If the teacher thinks that the class cannot deal with these two elements at one time, then s/he should choose content which does not include possessive adjectives.

3. Gather any props or realia that might help make the situation seem more realistic.

4. In the class, set the scene, with props if any.

5. Enact the scene with the class.

Follow-up

After doing a natural action dialog, you will often find it beneficial to do a TPR dictation. You may also find it worthwhile to do
some work on pronunciation.

Dictation

To practice spelling and writing, follow any of these exercises
with a simple dictation of sentences and questions you've been
practicing. Correct them together by having volunteers write
each line on the board: then go over them together, urging them
to check and correct their own papers. Point out unusual spel-
lings and teach spelling rules, such as dropping silent *e* (*rinse,
rinsing*) and doubling, or *not* doubling, final consonants (*stop,
stopping; eat, eating*) as you come to them. For more on TPR dictations see pp. 139-141.

Pronunciation Practice

Drill the students on the intonation of the lines of the dictation
as you point out the words, and/or drill them on difficult sounds,
contractions and/or elisions (slurring of words) which come up.

You are encouraged, of course, to devise your own natural action dialogs to suit the circumstances of your own classes. Keep
in mind that, in addition to being or — at the very least — seem-
ing natural, one of the ingredients of success is *making it fun and
interesting*, as opposed to mechanical. The focus should be on the
content, on what is occurring, on what is being accomplished, on
the task at hand. It is, of course, essential too that the activity be
designed so that it is appropriate to the level of the class and that
the circumstances of use be made obvious. The examples presented are mainly for the teaching of English. Many, but not all,
of them are transferable to other languages.

Action Role-Playing

In these freer exercises, only certain aspects of the situation
are suggested. The students must have had sufficient practice

with the vocabulary and structures which they need to communicate in their roles.

1. Both of you are about to go out and do some things. Talk to each other about what you're going to do. Then go out and do them and a few other things (in pantomime if necessary). Come back home and talk about what you did. (Pictures of places on wall and objects can be helpful.)

2. There are three people. Numbers One and Two run to the bus stop but just miss the bus that Number Three is driving. Apparently it's too late. They can't get to the places they were going to. They talk about what would and wouldn't have happened if they had caught the bus or hadn't missed it. Then, much to their surprise, Number Three drives up in the bus again and stops. They get on and go do the things they just said would happen. As in the above exercise, pantomime, wall pictures and objects may be used.

In a certain type of action role-playing, separate instructions are given to each of the participants:

3. Two students are given a number of objects to arrange on a table or desk. Neither one sees the written instructions which the other receives. One receives instructions to pile the objects up and get along well with the other one. The other is told to string the objects out and argue with the first one.

The above examples illustrate a framework for using TPR at any level to teach a wide variety of structures and vocabulary. TPR prepares students to perform role-playing with fuller emotion and to converse freely either with a ready-made dialog or one created by the students. TPR is "a 'happening' which is affecting their muscles and their senses. Totally experiencing the situation makes a strong impression and connects the words to something real, making learning much easier, more effective and more enjoyable for any student" (Romijn and Seely, 1988: x). Whether students are beginning or advanced, TPR enables learners to feel comfortable interacting with others in a second language and builds confidence for using the language outside the classroom (see Asher, 1982: 47-48).

Chapter 3:

Fluency and Connected Discourse

The term *fluency* is used in many ways. In this book the word *fluency* alone refers to the ability to express intelligibly in speech (without reading) what one wants or needs to without undue hesitancy or difficulty. The concept includes the ability to produce one sentence after another in "connected discourse." It does not refer to grammatical correctness or native-like pronunciation. (This is not to say that correctness and good pronunciation are not important or that they should never be worked on, just that they are not part of the concept of *fluency* as we use the word in this book.) What we might call "full fluency" is quite a different concept and is more or less equivalent to *full proficiency* in a language, indicating that a person who has achieved this is able to function at about the same level as most native speakers of the language. This is what is often meant when people say in English, "S/he is fluent in Navajo" or some other language. So, using the terms just described, *fluency* is an important *part* of *full fluency*, and it must somehow or other be developed by students.

The central question in regard to fluency is: ***How does the acquirer of a new language get everything s/he needs (words, structures, pronunciation) to the point where s/he can nearly always produce it readily when s/he wants or needs to?*** Certain factors appear to be essential to achieving fluency. The acquirer must:

- be very familiar with the material s/he wants/needs to produce.
- get plenty of practice in speaking without reading or rehearsal.

These two factors apply to vocabulary and structure. An acquirer can be very fluent with a minimal vocabulary and with few structures. The larger the vocabulary and the greater the number of structures, the fuller the expression of the speaker will be. The speech produced by a fluent speaker can range from native-like dominance to near unintelligibility. Among significant factors influencing intelligibility are pronunciation and intonation, mastery of structures, and extensiveness and accuracy of vocabulary.

Of course, we teachers must ask *what we can do to help students* get to the point where they can nearly always produce readily what they want or need to. There may be multiple answers to this question.

In language-teaching circles, the development of fluency and connected discourse currently consists almost entirely of what is known as "communicative activities," or activities that provoke students in one way or another to talk about a topic. We certainly agree that these are effective and useful means of developing fluency and connected discourse.

And we would like to propose some other types of activities that specifically promote fluency and connected discourse. The most significant by far of these is the network of activities used in TPR Storytelling. We suggest you read Chapter 4, "TPR Storytelling," to find out how all students develop fluency from early in the 1st year of high school through the 4th year; TPR Storytelling is also used in elementary school and middle school (see p. 84).

Here are two simple TPR activities (not from TPR Storytelling) that promote fluency and connected discourse:

- After practicing an action series by responding physically to commands several times, individual students give commands from the same sequence to the teacher without reading and without memorizing it word for word. They will be familiar with the logical sequence of events of the series, and their aim is to tell the teacher what to do, not to produce the exact wording they heard the teacher use. After a few students have given commands to the teacher, they can work in pairs. As usual, those who receive the commands perform them. It is important that they not read and that they not be corrected, for in this activity they are working on fluency and connected discourse in speaking, not in reading. As cues, they may look at pictures such as those in *Action English Pictures* (Takahashi and Frauman-Prickel, 1985; by the way, this book is usable with any language) (perhaps projected onto an overhead screen) or their own rough drawings, but no words. And they are not working on accuracy in this activity, though they may in others. They may even omit some steps. The important thing is to keep going, to produce one concept after another in a timely fashion. To avoid untimely delays from such an action as going to the door, the person performing the actions may pantomime all the actions instead of actually performing them.

- Similarly, but in a freer mode, students develop their own scenarios by giving commands. Of course, by the time they start doing this, they will have internalized a fair amount of the target language, at least, say, 100 words, probably more.

They probably will have begun to give single commands. Props, or realia, and illustrations on the walls serve as stimuli. At first and at other times it is wise to assign a topic; for instance, "Tell your partner to go to the bank and do some things there," or "Tell your partner to do some things that include using a towel." Simpler yet, just indicate a thing or a place or a person, such as a policewoman, and let it take off from there. In this instance, one student tells another to do various things in regard to the policewoman, for example:
- Wave to the policewoman.
- Say hello to the policewoman.
- Throw an apple to the policewoman.

The first time or two this activity is employed the teacher should demonstrate, giving the commands to an individual him- or herself. Then, one at a time, a few students can tell the teacher and other students. After that it can be done in pairs. The first attempts by students may be limited to as few as two or three commands. You may gradually expand the number of commands that students are expected to produce until it ceases to matter. With children through high school it is generally best to have them all performing at their desks; see the section on classroom management on page 161.

This activity may later be used with tenses, so that the speaker tells a story and the performer acts it out. And there may be two or more performers. It is best, however, to start with commands. And it is important to use activities that encourage students to find their own ways of expressing their ideas.

There are 3 essentials that are worth keeping in mind:
- The activities must *not* push them beyond their level.
- There should be no correcting or even self-correcting.
- Only the target language should be used in the activity.

The activities suggested here are monologues in which only one person speaks; this promotes connected discourse. If two people speak, the discourse is interrupted. (NOTE: The previous four sentences are based on ideas developed by Zev bar-Lev, Professor of Linguistics at San Diego State University, in the method he calls SILL, or Sheltered Initiation Language Learning. A key activity of the method is the "talkathon," in which learners speak without preparation in the target language for a given period of time for the purpose of developing fluency. There is no correction or self-correction. The talkathon is used even at the very beginning with very simple structures.) Remember that fluency and connected discourse develop over time. Once they have begun to do activities that promote fluency, students should continue to do them frequently.

Chapter 4:

TPR Storytelling

How can we language teachers help our students to achieve a reasonable degree of fluency at any particular level of language study? If you have heard the speech of high school students who have learned for even a few months through the approach named TPR Storytelling (also known as TPRS), you are likely to think about fluency in entirely different ways from before. Even the least talented students who have learned a language through TPR Storytelling achieve considerable fluency. (Please see the first paragraph in Chapter 3, "Fluency and Connected Discourse," above on page 35 for an explanation of what we mean by *fluency*.) Leading language acquisition expert Stephen Krashen of the University of Southern California says, "TPR Storytelling is much better than anything else out there."

My (Contee's) introduction to TPR Storytelling occurred at the annual conference of the California Foreign Language Teachers' Association (CFLTA, now known as the California Language Teachers' Association (CLTA)) which took place in Modesto in late April, 1992. Blaine Ray had with him two of his first-year high school Spanish students. On several occasions he asked them to perform, and they performed astoundingly well in front of 60-80 language teachers. The most convincing demonstration was when he asked the young lady, whom he called "Princesa," if she knew the story "Little Red Riding Hood." She said she did. Had she ever heard it in Spanish? No. Ray said, "O.K. I'll give you 5 minutes to get ready. You can draw some pictures as cues if you want to. In 5 minutes you can tell the story in Spanish. O.K.?" She said, "O.K.," and remained seated facing the audience while Ray went on addressing the teachers. 5 minutes later he said to her, "O.K. Ready?" She stood up and told the story in Spanish with some pauses and *uh*'s and *um*'s. She didn't know the word for *wolf*, so she substituted the word for *dog*. She told the story quite well with little preparation. She didn't use any pictures as cues. She had had about 7 full months of 55-minute Spanish classes (taking time out for vacations and holidays) for a total of about 140-150 55-minute hours. Ray said that both she and "Guapo" (handsome), the young man with her, were among his best students. He also said that even his "F students," the ones who don't do a lot of the work that is required of them, are also able to tell stories with some facility!

TPR Storytelling came into being as Blaine Ray, a high school Spanish teacher working in Ontario, Oregon, was experimenting with TPR in about 1987. It continues to develop at the time that this book goes to press as Ray teaches at Stockdale High School in Bakersfield, California. Ray had found TPR to be especially effective for aural comprehension. He found that, after using it with beginners for about a month, his students began to get restless. After trying a number of solutions to get his students to talk in some satisfactory way, he hit upon what has become TPR Storytelling. Asher makes several laudatory references to this approach in the 5th edition of his *magnum opus* on TPR, *Learning Another Language Through Actions* (1996). In his latest new work, *The Super School*, in a section entitled "What Can Be Done to Accelerate Production," the answer that he gives is Blaine Ray's TPR Storytelling. He says, "Rapidly, story by story, students are amazed to discover that they can express themselves in speech ... and writing" (pp. 13-8 and 13-9, 1995).

How It Works — From the Beginning

A beginning course in TPR Storytelling starts with what might be called "classical TPR." The teacher gives a command and performs the corresponding action to demonstrate the meaning of it. Then the teacher gives the command to the students, and the students move in response to it. The students are exposed to no more than three new words at a time. When all students can respond readily to the first three words, three more are introduced. When the students can deal with the second three well, the previous three are used along with them. When all six are being used smoothly, three more are introduced, and so on.

Already in this early stage *hand TPR* is being used. This is simply the use of gestures or hand signs to represent words or concepts. This significant innovation of Ray's — used along with whole-body TPR and other real movements — allows virtually all vocabulary to be internalized by means of TPR. (For further details on hand TPR, see pp. 43-48.) Ray will usually enhance the internalization process by mentioning mnemonic associations in the first language, such as:

- English "hunt the dog" for German *Hund* (dog)
- "buy a cow fin" for German *kaufen* (buy)
- "now, man, to gnaw" for French *maintenant* (now)
- "look for *sh* and share *sh*" for French *cherche* (look for)
- "call Roto-Rooter for a broken pipe" for Spanish *roto* (broken)
- "sop pot, oh, on your shoe" for Spanish *zapato* (shoe)
- Spanish "compra un baile" (buy a dance) for English *buy*
- French "joue s'il te plaît" (please) for English *play*

Students are encouraged to come up with their own associations. Sometimes they are better than the teacher's; these are gratefully and graciously accepted. If there is the slightest doubt that any student is not getting the meaning of a new vocabulary item without translation, then a quick translation is given orally. Ray points out that there are two times when a student is not benefiting from what s/he is hearing:

1. when it's not in the target language and

2. when it's not understood

Paradoxically, the surest way to make it understood is to give a quick translation. Then you can carry on, confident that everyone can follow and is acquiring the new vocabulary. (See "Ways and Means of Getting Across Meaning" on pp. 26-28.)

In addition to this "classical" process, soon after the beginning the teacher throws in some questions that can be answered with a single word, like this:

Grab a cat and put it on your head. Is the cat on your head or book?

The class or an individual answers, "Head," just a one-word answer.

After about a month, the students are so familiar with a significant repertoire of vocabulary that they are ready to start making the transition from the early-production stage to a fuller production stage. The teacher starts telling "mini-stories," and the students start *retelling* them. For example, after the students have used pantomime and gestures in response to commands enough times to internalize the words *have/has, cat, in, chair, run away, look for, everywhere, come back, sit down* and *asleep*, the teacher may tell this mini-story:

> Tammy has a cat in the chair. The cat runs away. Tammy looks everywhere for the cat. She comes back and sits down. Oh! The cat is asleep in the chair.

Mini-stories should contain some element of surprise, something to catch the interest of students. See pp. 50-52 for more ideas about what the optimal elements of a mini-story are.

Before telling the mini-story, the teacher picks out some actors/actresses to perform the story as it is being told. The actors/actresses are chosen for their abilities to act, for their lack of inhibition and for their willingness to perform. Some students enjoy doing this more than others, and usually it is obvious who they are. Students who are embarrassed or don't want to do it shouldn't be made to. The whole class enjoys such performances and remembers them well. They also help students to remember the words. The teacher often refers back to the mini-stories, since they are dramatic events that stand out for students.

In this case, an actress takes the part of Tammy (or in fact may be named Tammy, making her an integral part of the story), and an actor or actress takes the part of the cat. When the actors/actresses are ready in front of the class, the teacher tells the story, and they act it out. Everyone else observes with fascination. Everybody enjoys the performance/narration. This is no exaggeration; they really do.

The next step is for a few students to retell the mini-story. The first time this happens, the teacher asks for volunteers or chooses students who clearly would be able to do this comfortably and well. In addition or as another option, once the class is accustomed to mini-stories, everyone in the class can retell the story in pairs or small groups simultaneously. Mini-stories are retold from memory, never from the written word.

Notice that the students do not repeat the words of the mini-story after the teacher. Why? For two reasons: (1) because they don't need to; they are so familiar with the vocabulary and (2) because they are relating the story however they want to, not reciting a text. In the rare event that they cannot retell a mini-story, the reason is almost certainly that they have not yet internalized the vocabulary they need to tell the story. In this event, the teacher discovers that s/he must now do some more work on that vocabulary with hand TPR (see p. 41 and pp. 43-48) and/or remind students of mnemonic associations.

Also notice that they are not expected to produce everything perfectly in order to get across the ideas. The "mistakes" of 1st-year students are not corrected. This is a developmental stage in which they are expected to start to develop fluency by saying what they can, *not* parroting or repeating word for word and *not* reading. (For more about correcting, see "Why Not To Correct Students," pp. 62-64; for more about mini-stories, see pp. 50-63.)

These activities of the pre-production and early-production stages go on for about fifty minutes a day for five weeks. During this period students are internalizing the material that they are hearing and responding to physically.

One thing that is noticeably absent in this "classical" use of TPR is role reversal, in which students freely give commands to the teacher and to other students. Ray has not found this to be effective. So he uses "role reversal" *briefly* just once or twice in the prestorytelling stage and never after that. He points out that some American high school students, some 9th-graders in particular, tend to ridicule others when they freely command them. This is a behavior he prefers to avoid, especially since he sees very little pedagogical benefit in role reversal.

After this foundation is laid, Ray moves into full-blown storytelling. In most storytelling in language study the students are just listening to understand. With TPR Storytelling, all students actually learn to tell stories, and they create and tell their own stories. Ray's and his co-authors' stories, as well as those devised by students, generally contain some amusing elements, often even zany elements. Nearly always they contain surprises. They are engaging and fun.

Learning to Tell a Story — Step by Step

STEP ONE (of ten) in learning to tell a story is the internalization of the vocabulary. While all steps are important, this one is perhaps the one that is most critical. Even slower students who have thoroughly internalized the vocabulary find it is not difficult to accomplish the other steps and to tell stories.

The internalization of vocabulary continues to happen three words at a time, as mentioned above. From the time that the learning of the first full-length story begins, hand TPR — due to its efficiency — is the main vehicle for accomplishing internalization of vocabulary; everyone can do it at their seats.

Here are a few examples of hand TPR:

- Holding one hand horizontally face up at waist level and moving the other in a petting motion face down above it can be used to represent *cat*.

- One or both thumbs down can represent *bad*.

- To teach *it's raining* (*está lloviendo*) you can raise one hand or both and extend your fingers downwards while you shake them lightly as if to give the impression that water is falling from them.

Any sign can be chosen to represent any concept. Preferably there is some sort of logical and obvious connection between the sign and the concept. For the purposes of TPR Storytelling, the signs don't have to be retained by students (or teacher) beyond the time that the students internalize the vocabulary of a given story. The signs are a means to the end of internalizing that vocabulary.

Even structure words like *between* and *when* can be "TPR'd" this way — and abstractions like *philosophy* and *martyrdom*.

The stories in *Look, I Can Talk!* (1990) (the first-year book in Ray's TPR Storytelling series) range in length from 17 to approximately 35 sentences. Let's take a look at how a few words are internalized for one of the stories. There are 18 words listed in the vocabulary for "The Clothing Store," which is the fourth story in the book. The first three words are *beautiful, buy* and *clothing*. Here is the entire story (p. 28):

> Travis and Kim are walking along a street. They look down and find a pile of money. They say, "Great, let's go to a clothing store." They go into a clothing store.

Travis goes to the section of the store that has boys' clothing. He sees some pants that he likes. He tries them on. He says, "I want them." He tries on a shirt and some socks. He tries on a suit. He then tells the clerk, "I want the suit, the shirt, and the socks." Next, he goes to the shoe department. He tries on some shoes and says, "I want these shoes."

Kim goes to the girls' clothing department. A clerk there helps her. She tries on a beautiful dress. She says, "I want it." She tries on a blouse, a skirt, and some pants. She tells the clerk that she wants the blouse, the skirt, and the pants.

The clerk gives them the bill for the clothes. The clothes cost $295. They give him the pile of money. He counts the money. There is only $100. Kim says, "We will be right back. We will go find $200 more."

The teacher says the *first* word, "beautiful," and gets the meaning of this word across to the class quickly and clearly in some way. (See "Ways and Means of Getting Across Meaning" on pp. 26-28.) Then immediately s/he says the word again and follows it right away by using hand TPR to sign or gesture it. The sign for *beautiful* could be made by putting both hands six to nine inches in front of the chest with the fingers facing the chest and then circling both hands simultaneously upwards, then outwards and then moving them back down and in towards the body. This might be accompanied by a smile, since beautiful is a pleasant concept. Then the teacher says "beautiful" again, and the students respond physically with the sign.

The teacher introduces the *second* word, *buy*, in the same way — saying the word, getting the meaning across, saying the word again, then making the corresponding sign. The sign for *buy* could be made by holding one hand parallel to your stomach with the thumb slightly separated from the palm, then bringing the fingers of the other hand down into the space between the thumb and the palm of the first hand as if they are grasping bills from a wallet and pulling them out and giving them to buy something (see the illustration by Cherie Hearne on the next page). As before, after the introduction of the word, its meaning and the sign, the teacher says the word, "buy," again and the students make the sign in response.

TIPS:

- In cases of alternate forms like the feminine *belle* and the masculine *beau* (beautiful) in French, it is wise to present each form and to do so in context, for example, *un beau chat* and *une belle chatte*. They are presented separately one after the other, but the same sign or gesture is used for both. In practicing after the presentation, the teacher says one at a time, not both, for the students to respond to physically. Joe Neilson, one of Ray's co-authors, points out that contextualizing the alternate forms really helps students to grasp the usage of each form.

- The same goes for synonyms like *carro* and *coche* (Spanish for *car*).

- The situation is similar for verb forms, e.g., the forms *catch*, *caught* and *catches* can all be represented by the same catching motion. When it comes to distinguishing tense and person, some other signs may be used, either by themselves or along with the catching motion. See pp. 114-115 for ways to do this.

Then, immediately the teacher says the *first* word, "beautiful," and the students make the sign. The teacher follows it up right away by saying the *second* word, "buy," again, and the students make the sign. And so on, back and forth, with just the two words and their corresponding signs two or three times more — not many. With just two words and two signs there is normally no problem for anyone. Students are encouraged to "cheat," if they haven't made the connection between the word and the action, by looking at other students. The teacher performs the action again only if necessary.

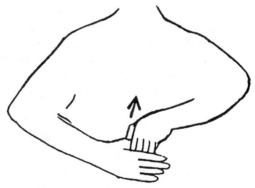

TIP: Blaine Ray suggests painting the picture in words or telling a little story about the gesture used. This speeds up the process of getting the meaning across. The more "hooks" students have for the meaning of a word, the quicker they grasp it and the firmer the grasp. And some who don't get it one way, will get it another. In the example of *buy* above, he tells students that the first hand is the wallet and the other hand is taking money out of it. Using mini-stories is especially advised in any case where the concept you are teaching might be not be totally clear to students, recommends Joe Neilson.

As soon as it is clear that every student is responding quickly and easily to both words, the teacher introduces the *third* word, *clothing*. The sign for *clothing* could be made by simply tugging at a couple of pieces of clothing, one above the waist, the other below, with one hand or both. In this case the sign and the meaning would be conveyed together.

Now there are three vocabulary items, each with its corresponding sign. The teacher says them several times, one at a time, mixing the order, until all students can give the appropriate sign without hesitation immediately after hearing each item. Sometimes s/he gives all three quickly one after the other — Ray calls these "chain commands" — and then the students make the corresponding signs in the same order. The order is varied. For variety, the teacher switches back and forth between chain commands and single commands. Also, s/he alternates between commands given to the whole class and ones given to individual students.

Then the teacher tells the students to close their eyes. S/he continues saying the three words, mixing them, and the students keep on making their physical responses — again, until everybody is able to respond readily to every item. At any point where any student appears to be having difficulty, the teacher stops and goes back and repeats whatever step or steps may be needed. Then s/he continues on until it is clear that everyone is able to respond quickly with their eyes closed.

TIP: Signs from American Sign Language can be used. ASL dictionaries can be helpful in finding good signs. A couple of good ones are listed in the bibliography. An example of the use of ASL is the sign for the word *woman*:

> Make a fist with the outermost joint of your thumb resting on your forefinger and the top of your thumb sticking up. Move your fingernails and thumb down along your jaw almost to your chin.
>
> One advantage of using ASL is that the teacher doesn't have to make up a sign for each word. Another is that the students not only learn words in the target language but also ASL words, or signs.

Before proceeding to the second set of three vocabulary items, it is *crucial* to check on some of the weaker students, those in the lowest 40% of the class, to make sure they have grasped each of the first three words. If the slowest students are getting it, obviously everybody is. The teacher does a spot check, saying several of the new words one at a time to one student in the target language and having him or her give each one back immediately in his or her first language. This translation check erases any doubt of possible confusion. If hand TPR is used instead to check internalization, some students may be able to make the sign readily without actually knowing the meaning of the word or the sign. If the teacher does not know the first language of the learner, of course the translation check cannot be used; another way of checking is necessary. You can use objects, pictures, actions; but to avoid possible misinterpretation, you must be sure whatever you use is clear and obvious.

> TIP: Since the slower students are likely to always be the same ones, the teacher theoretically might be constantly "badgering" the same individuals. With good rapport and sensitivity by the teacher to this possibility, students can actually feel they are receiving helpful attention rather than being badgered. If a student doesn't want to be continually assessed in this way, you should of course choose someone else.

When all students respond readily to the three words, three more words are taught in the same way while the first set is excluded for the time being. After the second set of three new words are internalized, they are mixed in with the three previous words, and the six are practiced together, first with eyes open, then with eyes closed. It is important at each juncture to check on the slower students to make sure every student is getting every item. As the repertoire of vocabulary for the story grows, some learners will have a little more trouble sorting items out. So, it takes a little longer to do the necessary practice for 15 words than it does for six.

Off and on throughout this process of internalizing the vocabulary, the teacher is doing **FOUR KEY THINGS** that enliven the process, make it fun, keep the students on their toes and make them want to understand and know what's going on :

1. Throwing in *novel commands*, saying odd or crazy things like "Buy the store" or "Eat the clothing."

2. *Asking students personalized questions* — questions about something in their world: themselves, their lives, their opinions. The best topics are those that really grab the students' attention, for example ones about a student in the class, about some place in town that students frequent, about controversial matters in the school like whether you can wear a hat in class, about local and school sports teams. While some questions are directed to individuals, most are put out for everyone to consider and anyone to answer. Questions must be carefully tailored to the level of the students, so that they will both understand the question immediately and be able to answer it without difficulty. The simplest questions for students to answer are:

   - *yes/no* questions, such as:
     Is the 49ers' *clothing* red?
       •answer: Yes *or* no.
   - choice questions with *or*, in which students choose between two alternative words which they hear in the question, such as:
     Is Bob's car *beautiful*, or is Bob's shoe *beautiful*?
       •answer: (His) car *or* (his) shoe.
   - questions that require a short answer but no verb, with *who, what, which, which one, how much, how many, how old* or *where*, such as:
     Samantha, where do you *buy* your shoes?
       •answer: (At) Smith's.

Notice that the students don't necessarily produce the new vocabulary word themselves. As they understand the questions and respond to them, they get comprehensible input in context and practice the production of simple answers. Any answer is acceptable, as long as the content of it is appropriate.

At a higher level, using the same vocabulary as examples, the teacher might ask questions that are more sophisticated in vocabulary, structure and/or length and that might require longer answers and/or a verb; the answer would not be provided in the question:

- Who's the most *beautiful* woman you know?
  - answer: María (is) (the most *beautiful* woman I know).
- How do you like Bob's *clothing*?
  - answer: (It's) very nice *or* I like it (a lot).
- Marianne, why did you buy those *shoes*?
  - answer: Because they're cool.

Occasionally the teacher asks a question that students don't understand. Rather than belabor the question, the teacher can immediately substitute a lower-level question that the students can get easily and respond to quickly. (For more on this, see Activity 4 on pp. 68-70. TPR expert Berty Segal Cook (a.k.a. Berty Segal) recommends using four levels of questions in early production stages; see pp. 119-120.)

3. Utilizing *mini-stories* as described above on pp. 42-43 and below on pp. 53-62. ***Ray believes that it is mainly through the mini-stories that students acquire accurate fluency***. Learning a full-length story entails learning several mini-stories as part of the process. They are used as building blocks — smaller units which help students to master vocabulary and structure in context. Usually 6-8 mini-stories are learned during the learning of a single full-length story, though there may be as few as 4 or as many as 10. The actual number used depends on:

   a. how many new vocabulary items are in the full-length story.

   b. the level of the new grammatical material, if there is any, in the new story.

   c. the amount of previously used vocabulary and grammatical material the teacher believes the class should put into use again.

   d. the length of the mini-stories; in general a mini-story used for this purpose contains 6-10 new vocabulary items; if it contains new grammar that is difficult, it might contain no new vocabulary.

It is most important to make the mini-stories interesting to the class — the story itself should be interesting and the performances by students of it should be too.

Mini-stories are always acted out while the teacher tells them. The manner in which they are acted out is extremely important. Even an interesting story can be made lifeless by a lifeless performance. Exaggeration in both gesture and voice inflection helps to instill life into a story and make a strong impression on the whole class, thereby making it much easier for them to remember the story. In order to be sure the enactment is sufficiently dramatic, the teacher sometimes has to coach the actors by demonstrating with, for example, gigantic gestures and overdone voice inflection. After a mini-story is acted out at least once, it is retold by students from memory, never from the written word. For example:

> Nicole finds a big pile of money on the street. She wants a blouse. She is walking to a clothing store. She finds a beautiful blouse on the street too. And she sees a friend, Ron. Ron is very hungry. She gives all the money to Ron, and she goes home with the blouse.

This mini-story is an example of what a mini-story should be. It:
- is interesting.
- contains a surprise or two.
- utilizes exaggeration; some ways to exaggerate in a story are: size, time, money, speed, stamina — actually anything can be taken to a ridiculous extreme.
- is brief or of appropriate length for the level of the class (some mini-stories are much longer, even over 100 words; in general the shorter the

mini-story, the easier it is to deal with; mini-stories that are long or overloaded with new material may not hold students' attention throughout the time they are learning them); if you are not sure whether there is too much new material, it is best to reduce the amount, erring perhaps on the side of simplicity.

- consists of sentences which are appropriate in complexity and difficulty to the level of the class.
- highlights a limited number of new vocabulary words.
- is relevant to students, about a student or two in the class, Nicole and Ron; this heightens interest.
- says something nice about a student, Nicole; this strengthens rapport in the whole group.

When mini-stories are used to practice something grammatical, such as a tense, there may be no new vocabulary included in them. This happens particularly when a new grammatical point is a major one and requires special attention. Here is a mini-story in the future tense:

Tri will come to my house. He will go in quietly. My mother will scream. Tri will run away.

Even where more sophisticated vocabulary is being practiced, the same criteria listed above should be used. Here's an example:

Paul has one serious *vice*. He spends money. He goes shopping and spends 58,000 dollars. He goes to Rebecca's house and gives everything to her. Rebecca likes everything and starts to cry *uncontrollably*.

Ray has written three books of mini-stories for teachers (the first with Joe Neilson) (Neilson and Ray, 1996; Ray, 1996a; and Ray, 1996b), each one with several stories based on each of the main stories in the corresponding textbooks. There are three videos which demonstrate how to teach mini-stories — *Blaine Ray's TPR Storytelling Workshop Video* (Ray, 1997) and a set of two *¡Mírame, puedo hablar! Mini-Stories Videos* (Ray and Neilson, 1998).

4. Stimulating *class discussions*. Early on these may be very brief, and students will not be able to express much. So it is the teacher's job to ask provocative or controversial questions that allow students to answer at the level that they are able to, as in no. 2 above. For example, a question like *Who pays for your clothes?* or *Do you pay for your clothes or do your parents?* is of personal interest to every high school kid and easy to answer with a word or two.

> TIP: In both (2) making vocabulary relevant and (3) using mini-stories, Ray makes a conscious effort to advertise the talents and good attributes of his students. He finds this an excellent way to establish or deepen rapport between himself and his students — a crucial element in learning in all classes. On occasions when one student puts down another, he talks to the offending student after class and points out that the rules of the game require praise, not ridicule.

These four keys continually maintain everybody's interest at a high level, students' and teacher's alike. The novel commands keep students wondering what's coming next; the situation is unpredictable. The questions with personalized vocabulary are real and deal with the students' own lives. The presentation of the mini-stories is captivating; the retelling of them is involving. The class discussions are on topics of real interest to everyone.

The procedures of Step One continue until all the vocabulary for the story has been internalized by the entire class. Ray believes that **deep internalization of words through** comprehensible input, especially **aural comprehensible input**, is essential if students are to be able to produce them in a timely manner in speech when they want and need to. This **is a key to fluency** that doesn't seem to have been recognized elsewhere in the language teaching field. It is not enough for students just to know the meaning of a word or to be able to translate it. They must become thoroughly familiar with it by means of classical TPR and/or other aural comprehensible input before they are ready to produce it readily in speech.

In the 2nd- and 3rd-year books (*Look, I Can Talk More!* (Ray et al., 1992) and *Look, I'm Still Talking!* (Ray and Neilson, 1993)) the first page of each chapter is entitled "Vocabulary" and has four comic-strip-style 4-panel "vocabulary picture mini-stories" which contain all the vocabulary just presented and internalized (see illustration by Christopher Taleck below from p. 13 of *Look, I'm Still Talking!*).

In the 2nd year, to internalize it just a little more thoroughly, before moving on to the second step, the teacher tells one of these vocabulary picture mini-stories, with actors/actresses acting it out, as above (p. 42 and pp. 51). Then several students retell it one by one, looking only at the pictures on the first page of the chapter or on the overhead screen. (Again, everyone may retell the story simultaneously in pairs.) After each of the four picture mini-stories has been retold, the students turn to the following page, where the vocabulary for each panel of every story is given. Below the vocabulary, for each story, are four lines on which students write sentences using the vocabulary to describe the panels and tell the story. Each of the four picture mini-stories is done in the same way. The writing is done as homework.

The 1st-year book has a picture for each vocabulary item instead of the picture mini-stories; at Stockdale High School, these pictures are no longer used as a teaching tool. Ray says that if and when the book is redone, he would like to replace the vocabulary items with picture mini-stories.

With the 3rd-year book the procedure is a little different. Rather than a list of the vocabulary on the page after the vocabulary picture mini-stories, there is a description of each panel. After internalizing the vocabulary of a mini-story through TPR, students read the description of each panel of the story. Then they tell the story from the pictures in the panels (not reading), as other students act it out.

At this point we move on to **STEP TWO** in learning to tell a story — the first telling of the story. But the teacher doesn't just tell the story. The telling is accompanied by a performance by some students who act it out. It is very important that the performance be very dramatic and make a strong impression, as mentioned above on p. 51. The rest of the class observes and listens. The telling and the performance are repeated usually one or more times, perhaps with different actors in each repetition, until all students are satisfied that they can follow the story easily. Each telling may be slightly different in details such as the exact choice of vocabulary and the stress used by the speaker, but the storyteller recounts the same events in every telling. The speed may increase in the later tellings. After the second or third telling, the dramatization is discontinued. Drawings on overhead transparencies or on the board or a poster — or those provided in the text — can be pointed to by the teacher to help students follow the story during the third, fourth and fifth tellings.

> TIP: A person can take the part of an *animal* or even of some large *things*, like a window (by forming a large hoop with the tips of one's hands and holding the hoop vertically for someone else to look through or throw something through). Sometimes two or more people can use their arms and be something, like a house or a section of a store.

STEP THREE in learning to tell a story consists of the teacher retelling the story event by event by questioning and prompting to elicit short oral responses about the story by students. This occurs in five ways, which are used one at a time in any order and afterwards can be mixed up (or, with groups that are advanced enough to handle them, the techniques may be mixed right away). The students answer freely without the teacher choosing anyone to answer, shouting out their answers, the idea being that every student can participate in helping to tell the story.

> *Technique 1.* The teacher asks yes/no questions and other questions that can be answered with just a word or two, like "Do they go into a clothing store?" and "What does he see?" The students answer, "yes" and "(some) pants." Some of these questions would begin with *what, who, where, when, which (one(s)), how much, how many* and *how.* (Notice that some questions with *how* would elicit longer, more complex responses.)
>
> *Technique 2.* The teacher says a sentence from the story with a mistake in it, such as "They find a pile of bananas."

The students shout out the correction, which may be a single word like "money" or may be a phrase like "a pile of money" or a whole sentence like "They find a pile of money."

Technique 3. The teacher pauses to leave a space at the end of a sentence in the story, as in "She tries on a beautiful ____." The students blurt out, "dress."

Technique 4. The teacher asks *or* questions such as "Do they have one hundred dollars or three hundred dollars?" The students respond, "one hundred dollars."

Technique 5. The teacher asks *why* questions like "Why does Travis go to the boys' clothing section?" This is a very simple question with an obvious answer, but the teacher should also ask questions to which the answer is not known, such as "Why are they walking along the street?" Usually many answers are possible to *why* questions, so the teacher should ask for several different answers, eliciting them from various students. This technique actually encourages students to interpret the story somewhat. The answers are likely to be a little longer than the ones students produce with the other techniques.

Again, afterwards these five techniques can be mixed as the teacher goes through the events of the story. What's happening with all of these techniques is that the students get a chance to play around with the content of the story. They're hearing it, considering it, producing bits of it.

An additional option between Steps 3 and 4: In *Chalk Talks* (Shapiro and Genser, 1994), a book about how to use simple drawings to stimulate speaking, Norma Shapiro suggests that students copy the drawings representing a story from the board or the overhead screen onto a piece of paper. Ray believes it would be counterproductive to have students copy the words of the story, because this would encourage them to memorize the words rather than describing the events as best they can from the picture cues or from their own memories of the events. That is to say, copying the words would discourage fluency and promote word-for-word memorization.

In *STEP FOUR* the teacher writes a list of **guide words** on the board or the overhead. Guide words are an innovation from Joe Neilson, who teaches Spanish through TPR Storytelling at Salpointe Catholic High School in Tucson, Arizona. They help boost the level of language of first-year students and help them to express themselves more smoothly. They are used extensively from the second year on, but only sparingly in the first year. In the first year they help students' production level by improving their mastery of selected vocabulary and idioms. They also help students to remember the sequence of events in a story. In the second, third and fourth years they have a significant positive effect on students' accuracy in speaking. Guide words are single words or, more often, combinations of words from the story which the teacher wants students to put into use as they tell the story. They are words or phrases that students are using for the first time, or they are ones which they haven't used much or which they have been using inadequately. For the most part they fall into the following categories:

1. They emphasize the grammatical point(s) of the story.
2. They emphasize certain new vocabulary items.
3. They provide ways for students to smoothly link one sentence to the next.
4. They are items that students would be likely to have trouble producing accurately or have had trouble producing well.

Only a few **guide words** are used **with first year stories** — usually 2 or 3, at the most 4 or 5. Two types of guide words (or phrases) are used in the first year: (1) ones the teacher wants to make sure that students start using, like *pile of money* (many students would be tempted to use just the single word *money* as they are telling the story) and (2) words like *while, when* and *that* which are used to link clauses to form longer sentences and make the flow of the language more natural. Using both of these types of guide words helps students to elevate the level of the language they produce. In "The Clothing Store" (pp. 44-45) the teacher might use only two or three items, for example, *while* and *pile of money*. The first sentence in the story, *Travis and Kim are walking along a street*, can be linked with the second, *They look down and find a pile of money*, by using *while*: *While Travis and Kim are walking along a street, they look down and find a pile of money*.

At least a couple of class sessions before asking students to use a new word like *while*, the teacher will have introduced it and the students will have practiced it on a few different occasions through TPR (with action, but not necessarily with commands). For instance, in introducing *while* in this earlier session, the teacher says (using the actual name(s) of the actor(s)/actress(es)), "While Sujatha is eating a hamburger, she hears an explosion." Sujatha pantomimes eating the hamburger while the rest of the class makes the sound effect. This same scenario is then repeated a few times with half the class taking the part of Sujatha and the other half making the sound effect, while the teacher says the sentence. This sentence and the dramatic experience that goes with it will then serve as a "memory hook" for the word *while* for the rest of the school year and even longer. (Whenever the teacher wants to remind the class of *while*, s/he begins to say this sentence — just "While Sujatha ..." — and it triggers the whole sentence and the concept in the minds of the students.) A few other *while* sentences are then presented and practiced in the same fashion, and the teacher provides a few more examples for comprehensible input without dramatization, in both cases with vocabulary that the class is already familiar with. *While* sentences are subsequently practiced in the same active way on at least one other occasion before *while* is used as a guide word with a story, so that the students are quite familiar with this new word and its use before they are expected to produce it as they tell a full-length story.

With these prior preparations having been made and after the completion of Step 3 above (pp. 55-56), the teacher writes the guide words *While Travis and Kim are walking* on the board or overhead for students to incorporate in their telling of this first-year story. The phrase *pile of money* is in the original story, so it needs no introduction at this point; it is just written on the board or overhead to remind students to use it.

The following mini-story (the guide words procedure is used with both full-length stories and mini-stories), presented here in both Spanish and English, contains more advanced material and serves as an example of how guide words are used in **Step 4 after the first year**. In it there are some irregular verbs (grammar point), there are object pronouns (another grammar point, which in this example might be considered more as a reminder than as a point to be focused on), there is a new expression or idiom (vocabulary), and there is an odd feminine word in Spanish (*foto*) and a tricky two-word verb in English (*screamed at*) (both good candidates for inaccurate production), all in context:

> María trajo una foto de su novio a la clase. La puso en su pupitre. Roberto la vio y la agarró. María le gritó. La profesora le dijo a ella, "¡Pon atención!" María la miró y Roberto comió la foto.

Mary brought a picture of her boyfriend to class. She put it on her desk. Robert saw it and grabbed it. Mary screamed at him. The teacher said to her, "Pay attention!" Mary looked at her, and Robert ate the picture.

The following guide words are written on the chalkboard or overhead for the Spanish or the English version of the story:

trajo	brought
una foto	put it
La puso	saw it
la vio	grabbed it
la agarró	screamed at him
le gritó	said to her
le dijo	Pay attention!
¡Pon atención!	looked at her
la miró	ate
la foto	

Notice that the object pronouns are listed in context along with their verbs and that in English the preposition part of two-word verbs is also given.

The above lists of guide words might seem excessively long, considering the length of the story, and in fact they might be. However, it is worthwhile noting that (1) the list is not so long, only 9 or 10 items (a full-length story has roughly 20-30 items and they are listed by paragraph; so that if there are 3 paragraphs in the story, the guide words for each paragraph are in a separate column or there is a line between the guide words for one paragraph and those for the next), (2) in order to tell the story a student must know more than what is in the list of guide words (s/he must know the story and must be able to assemble sentences), (3) the guide words are intended to be used only as an aid when needed by each teller (some students will need to look at some guide words, others at others, some at none), and (4) students know that they are only available temporarily and that they will have to tell the story without them very soon.

TIPS:

1. Neilson warns that, if too many of the words in a story are guide words, there is a tendency for some students to just read the list, filling in the gaps to complete the story.

2. It should be made clear to students that they are *telling* the story, not reading it, and that the guide words are there to help them when they need them. They should look at them only when they need to. Reminding them that soon they will be telling the story without access to the guide words should help get this point across. Otherwise, they will get the point "the hard way."

In **STEP FIVE** a student, one who the teacher knows can set a good example in telling the story, may tell the story, using the guide words as necessary. Other students may act out the story while the storyteller is narrating. Drawings on overhead transparencies or the board or a poster serve as cues to help remind the teller of the sequence of events. Whether this is done or not, all students work in pairs and tell the story to each other, making sure that they include the guide words in their telling. The correctness of other words in the story would *not* be dealt with during this process unless they caused misunderstanding.

An additional option between Steps 5 and 6: The whole class tells the story together as they follow the picture cues on the board, a poster or the overhead screen. This is likely to increase their confidence in telling it when they're doing it on their own. This should *not* involve repeating after the teacher and *should* allow for different ways to describe each event in the story. (Ray has not done this but sees no problem with it.)

STEP SIX is for one or two volunteers to retell the story. They have been practicing and usually several students are eager to do this.

STEP SEVEN: When the teacher thinks the students can tell the story well without seeing any words at all, s/he erases or removes all the guide words. One or two more students now tell the story for the whole class, looking at pictures if they like, but not words. If the teacher asks one or two of the weaker students to retell the story and they do so without difficulty, it is clear that the whole class can handle it and its contents well. This allows for a quick assessment of the class as a whole to find out whether the class needs further work on the material in the mini-story. Choosing weaker students to perform at this point is usually done only with mini-stories.

STEP EIGHT is for everyone to tell the story to partners or in small groups. Again, as they tell the story, they can use the drawings from the book or from the board, the overhead screen or a poster to remember the sequence of events. No guide words are in sight, and they should *not* be reading. Other members of the group may act out the events. At no time are students required to be perfect in grammar or pronunciation. They are expected to get the story across intelligibly. Nobody has to tell the story to the whole class. If desired, bonus points can be given to students who stay on task.

STEP NINE: After all the students have told the story in pairs without seeing any words, the teacher focuses on a few important items just a little more by telling several students, one at a time, to repeat certain parts of the story. For instance, s/he says in the target language, "Jan, repeat the part of the story with the words 'saw it' or 'Pay attention!' "

STEP TEN: Each and every student tells as much of the story as s/he can as fast as s/he can in 15 seconds. This is done one student after another — bang, bang, bang. Every student must be ready to go as soon as the previous one stops. The teacher or the last student who will do this watches the time and calls out "Next!" every 15 seconds. It doesn't matter how far each student gets; it's the effort that counts. This is a fluency exercise and is fun for everyone as the grand finale. For a class of 30 students it takes 7 1/2 minutes. This step is done only with full-length stories.

Steps 8 and 9 are sometimes omitted for mini-stories but never for full-length stories. It depends on whether the teacher feels that the students have acquired what they need to from working with a mini-story. As mentioned above on p. 50, usually 6-8 mini-stories based on one full-length story are done, though as few as 4 or as many 10 may be done.

Most students experience some difficulty when they tell the first full-length stories. The teacher should keep this in mind. After going through the whole process involved in learning to tell the first story, students begin to gain in confidence and facility in telling succeeding stories. In fact, after the beginning *even slow students find full-length stories are not difficult to tell if the vocabulary has been taught well and the above steps have been used.*

Another technique that is useful for variation after all students have told the story in pairs is a sequential telling of the story. One student tells a few sentences of the story from the beginning. Then the teacher tells another student to tell the following segment, then another and another, until the whole story has been told.

Telling a full-length story in a reasonably smooth manner demonstrates clearly that students can in fact talk the language to a certain rather impressive degree (the degree depends on the level of language of the story as well as the facility with which a student tells it). By telling a full-length story fairly well, students are telling whoever is listening, "Look, I can talk!" — which is the title of Ray's series of texts.

Why Not to Correct Students

One of the main aims of students telling stories is the development of free expression and fluency. It is important **not to correct them at all**. This is likely to inhibit their fluency and is unlikely to have any beneficial effect. Ideally, for the purposes of developing fluency, students don't even think of accuracy in grammar or pronunciation. They should have blind confidence in that what they say is fine. Correcting them or working on grammatical correctness or "good" pronunciation brings these matters to their attention and often inhibits fluent production. Lack of inhibition promotes fluency.

Ray's brand of storytelling provides a framework in which students can freely express meaning however they want to and are able to, at the same time that they continually acquire new elements of the target language. When they learn to retell a story, just how they formulate their sentences — what words and structures they choose to use as they retell the story — is up to them. And this is the way Ray looks at the skill of speaking. The choice of words and structures must be the speaker's. Otherwise the speaker is memorizing or parroting, not speaking.

Here is a **SUMMARY** of the above steps for learning to tell a story:

1. Internalization of vocabulary
2. First tellings of story by teacher, accompanied by student performances
3. Students help teacher retell story through:
   a. short-answer questions
   b. correcting teacher mistakes

    c. filling in pauses

    d. choosing between alternatives

    e. saying why things happen

4. Teacher writes guide words on board or overhead

5. Perhaps one student retells the story for whole class; then everyone practices in pairs with guide words in view

6. One or two volunteers retell story

7. Teacher removes guide words; one or two students retell without guide words

8. All students retell to partners

9. Several students retell specified parts of story

10. Every student tells as much of story as possible in 15 seconds

Grammar and pronunciation are developmental. They gradually develop as a learner progresses in vocabulary, in scope of aural comprehension, in fluent spoken expression, in reading comprehension, in fluent written expression. They are gradually acquired. They are not learned. So, in Ray's view, generally there is no use correcting grammar and pronunciation — until a student has reached a point when s/he is ready for a specific correction. Occasionally the teacher does make an "indirect correction" by restating correctly what a student has said in the target language without requiring or expecting him/her to repeat it back, giving the student timely comprehensible input, which the student may digest and which may at some later time affect output. "Quicker" students may put some of these indirect corrections to use immediately and continue to use them correctly — if they're ready for the particular correction.

Ray and Asher believe that beginning students don't have what Asher calls enough "attention units" available to process corrections. Their attention units are being used to get out the message they are conveying. Later on they think students are able to give attention to coaching for accuracy in grammar. In TPR Storytelling as practiced by Ray and his colleagues at Stockdale High School, such coaching begins sometime in the 2nd year with the correction of one single item (see below p. 74 in the section entitled "Accuracy in Production," pp. 72-76).

They rarely correct pronunciation or deal with it directly in any way. They feel that their students always pronounce adequately. The reason is that, before they ever say a word, they have heard it many times, become thoroughly accustomed to it and internalized it. Only in very special circumstances does the teacher help a student with pronunciation. If a student can hear well, s/he will nearly always pronounce intelligibly. The aim is not for students to speak with perfect pronunciation but rather for them to express themselves intelligibly and naturally.

After having worked with the target language for some time, students get used to many features of the language and may not have to hear a word many times before they can say it adequately. Often in this stage they "pick up" a word here and there the first or second time they hear it.

Ray recognizes that in some situations, such as Chinese adults learning English, it might be necessary to do some kind of direct work on pronunciation. In any class, a teacher may need to seat the hard of hearing at the front of the class.

Follow-Up Activities

There are a number of follow-up activities in which the students keep using the material of the story in a variety of ways. The order in which these are done is of little consequence. What is important is that everyone have a firm grasp of the vocabulary before doing them. If they do, they can do these activities well. Doing them strengthens their grasp on the material and provides them with several different ways to practice it. The following 8 activities are in each chapter of the 1st-year book:

Activity 1 — Reading Aloud. After they all tell the story, students read it out loud from the textbook. This is done in a variety of ways, sometimes in chorus, sometimes individuals reading to the whole class, sometimes students reading a sentence at a time one after another, sometimes with translation.

Activity 2 — Written Exercises. Following the written presentation of the story in the 1st-year textbook, there are reading and writing exercises of the usual sort: true/false, fill-in-the-blank, short-answer and sequencing. These all have to do with comprehension or production of meaning, not with correct form.

The 2nd-year book has more challenging written exercises. Here are the instructions for them:

1. Complete the sentences (about the main story).

2. Answer the questions in your own words (about the main story).

3. Write the story from a different point of view (e.g., in the *I* form rather than the *s/he* form). This is a very effective tool for the acquisition of verb forms (see also pp. 73 and item 6 on pp. 86-87).

4. Answer the personal questions (about yourself).

5. Write the story that the class makes up. (This is Activity 4 below on pp. 66-67.)

6. Make up a new ending for the main story.

7. Look at the 3rd and 4th drawings for this new story, and complete the story with some original drawings. Use at least 6 vocabulary words from this chapter. (There are six panels beneath these instructions, four of them blank; see illustration on the next page by Christopher Taleck from p. 60 of *Look, I'm Still Talking!*, Ray and Neilson, 1993.)

8. Write the story that you just drew above (in no. 7).

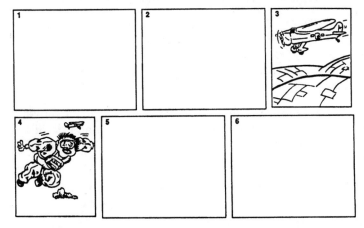

In the 3rd-year text nos. 2, 4, 7 and 8 of these types of exercises are used. The other written exercises at this level force students to think more than the other four in the 2nd-year text. The following are the instructions for these:

1. Answer the questions (about the main story) with two possibilities.
2. Points of view: Describe the following people or things from various points of view. Invent at least two characteristics for each description. Examples:
   - Describe the wild class from the point of view of the students. (p. 30)
   - Describe Pete's parents from Pete's point of view. (p. 18)
3. Read the situations and try to solve the problem. An example:
   - A girl just parachuted out of an airplane flying two miles high. She has forgotten how to operate her parachute. What can she do to solve this small problem? (p. 19)
4. Invent a problem and then write three possible solutions.
5. Invent a story with 6 actions and then draw the pictures. The story should include at least 10 vocabulary words from this chapter. (Six blank panels are given below these instructions.)
6. Write the story that you drew above (in no. 5).

Activity 3 — Writing the Story. For the first several stories, students write out a copy of the story they have just read. Later in the first year everyone writes the story out in their own words, not copying. This generally is not done after the 1st year. It may be a homework assignment.

Activity 4 — Oral Questions. The teacher has a conversation with the class in which the students as a group add details to the story. For example, in "The Clothing Store" (above on pp. 43-44) the teacher asks some questions like these:

1. How old are Kim and Travis?
2. Are they friends or boyfriend and girlfriend?
3. What are they wearing?
4. Is Kim wearing a blue shirt?
5. Is it old?
6. Is it dirty or clean?
7. Is Travis tall or short?

8. Do they find more money?
9. How much?
10. Where?
11. Do they buy everything they want?
12. Do they buy the pants, the shirt, the socks, the suit, the shoes for Travis?
13. Do they buy the dress, the blouse, the skirt, the pants for Kim?
14. Do they buy anything else?
15. How do they get home after they finish buying their new clothes?
16. Why doesn't Kim buy shoes?

These questions are formulated by the teacher while s/he is keeping in mind:

1. What vocabulary the students are able to recognize.
2. The level of their speaking ability. For example, with low beginners who haven't been creating their own sentences much yet, the teacher will use entirely yes/no questions (like nos. 4, 5, 8, 11, 12, 13 and 14); choice questions (mostly with *or*) (like nos. 2, 6, 7, 12 and 13) and questions with *who, what, which, which one, how much, how many, how old* and *where* (like nos. 1, 3, 9 and 10). These are questions that require only a single word to answer and usually no verb. Often the answer is contained in the question, as in nos. 2, 6, 7, 12 and 13. With students who have begun to formulate their own sentences, the teacher will ask more questions with the question words *how* and *why* that are likely to require longer answers (like nos. 15 & 16, which would probably not be asked as early as the 4th story but are given here as examples of questions that can elicit longer answers from students when they have developed some ability to create sentences). (See also item 2 on pp. 54-55 and the description of Berty Segal Cook's (a.k.a. Berty Segal) four levels of questions on pp. 119-120.)

Students take notes during this activity; they know they will have a quiz on it the next day. Some totally new vocabulary items creep into these question-and-answer sessions. For instance, say the class has not yet had the word *live* at all. The teacher might say, "I

67

live in Paradise [a place everybody knows]," and then ask, "Where does Kim live?" A few little items like this may be "picked up" by students and produced in the retelling that follows. After the story has been expanded in this session, the teacher asks two or three or four students to tell this more detailed version of it in the target language. Sometimes s/he calls on 20 to 30 students each to tell a 15-second segment of the story one after the other, one picking up where the previous one leaves off.

Activity 5 — Oral Questions to Develop Other Versions. The student books contain, in addition to the original story, a couple of other versions of the same story presented in picture form only. These versions are also topics of conversation. They are displayed with an overhead projector or on a poster, or they are drawn on the board. In a manner like that used to expand the original story in Activity 4 above, the class develops each story with considerable detail in response to questions asked by the teacher, especially *why* questions as soon as the class is able to handle them.

Activity 6 — Pair Work: New Stories. The students work in pairs to make up a new story in which they use *mostly the same vocabulary*. They may use their native language as they prepare their story. They make their own little drawings on a piece of paper as cues. They should not write words on this paper, because they are not going to read the stories; they're going to tell them. They practice them a little immediately and a little the next day. Each pair chooses actors/actresses from their other classmates to act out the story. Then each student in every pair tells their story to the class as the selected actors/actresses listen and perform. After the first teller in a pair has finished, the second one tells the story again. This time the actors/actresses switch roles, so that each one acts to different words than s/he did the first time the story was told.

Activity 7 — Homework: Writing New Stories. As homework students write their own new stories also based on the original, i.e., with mostly the same vocabulary. They turn this in, and the teacher reads it to see how the students are doing, but s/he doesn't correct it or grade it. Students don't tell this story.

Activity 8 — Mini-Stories. At the end of each chapter there are ten mini-stories based on the material in the original story. They serve as examples of mini-stories which might be used in Step One (pp. 44-54) of the six steps for learning to tell a story. (They are also examples for the teacher to base mini-stories on in the pre-storytelling phase (pp. 40-43) in the first 5 weeks.) Students read them just for fun and to understand them. They serve as more comprehensible input. They can also be used with the following steps:

1. The teacher tells a mini-story. (The students are *not* reading.)
2. Every student quickly makes his/her own *simple* drawings of the mini-story.
3. Students retell the mini-story from their drawings (*not* from the words in the book). A few may do this for the whole class, and/or they may all do it simultaneously in pairs.

Here are some examples of the 120 mini-stories in the 1st-year book (Ray, 1990):

1. The monkey has a house. He is sleeping in a bed. The cow goes to the monkey's house. The cow screams. The monkey wakes up. The monkey is mad. (Chapter 2, p. 16)
2. Nick's mom asks him why he has so much money. He says that he has a rich friend who gave him a million dollars. She says Nick can keep the money if he gives her $1,000. (Chapter 5, p. 40)
3. Fred marries the waitress and stays on the moon. He buys a moon house. They have moon children. He never goes back to Earth. (Chapter 8, p. 64)
4. Jim tells his parents that a bird came into his room and took one of his records. He ran after the bird for two hours. The bird finally dropped the record and he got it back. His parents were glad he was being honest. (Chapter 11, p. 88)

Activity 9 — Vocabulary Review. This important activity is not in the student book. At some point after all students have retold the story, all the vocabulary of the lesson is reviewed. This is done in three ways, which are all used throughout the 4-year program. Each is used on a different day, so that there are always three vocabulary reviews:

- 8 1/2" x 11" picture flash cards are shown one after another by the teacher, usually for the whole class to respond to. The students produce the appropriate word orally in the target language. Notice here that they *are* asked to produce, but only after they have already retold the story.

Sometimes the flash cards are used in a game invented by Spanish and ESL teachers Scott Peterson and Lori French of Arvin High School in Arvin, California, in which the first student to call out the word that is depicted on a card flashed by the teacher receives the card. At the end, the two students who have the most cards come forward. The teacher gathers up all the cards and stands behind the two contestants so that they cannot see her/him. S/he holds up each card one at a time so that the rest of the class *can* see them. Members of the class call out hints in the target language. Whichever of the two contestants "gets" the word first receives a point. Great fun!

- Hand TPR is used as it is when comprehension of various items is checked in Step One of the initial internalization of the vocabulary (pp. 44-54). This is for recognition; the students give a hand signal upon hearing a word; they don't speak.

- Translation; the teacher says a word in the target language; the students give an oral translation immediately in their first language; again, this is for recognition.

Of course in all three ways of reviewing, if weakness appears on certain items, these are reviewed further. Notice that vocabulary is presented and/or reviewed in a variety of ways:

- Hand TPR
- Mnemonic associations
- Pictures
- Translation

This allows students who have different learning or acquisition styles to take advantage of them. For most students it is likely that the various ways reinforce one another.

The Day-by-Day Schedule for the First Year

In the first year, all the work done on one story takes place over a period of two weeks. The students use and reuse the material in a variety of ways. They're building fluency with it. And the variety keeps them interested and avoids "adaptation" (see pp. 159-160). Below is a schedule that indicates roughly what is done day by day in the two weeks of 55-minute classes that are spent working on a story in the first year:

Day-by-Day Schedule for the First Year

1st Week

Monday		As much of Step One for learning to retell the story as possible
Tuesday	25 min.	Review and continuation of Step One
	20 min.	Steps 2-6
	10 min.	The preparatory part of Activity 6 — making up stories in pairs, drawing cues, practicing a little
Wednesday		Activity 6 — students telling their stories as others act them out
Thursday	15 min.	Review of vocabulary with hand TPR
	40 min.	Activity 4
Friday	20 min.	Quiz on the story created in Activity 4, with open notes
	35 min.	Activity 1

2nd Week

Monday	25 min.	Internalization of 10 supplemental vocabulary words, as in Step One. These words and those internalized on the next two days are first-year words that are included in stories. After they are internalized, they are used in various contexts from this time on.
	30 min.	Activity 5 with Version A of the story
Tuesday	25 min.	Internalization of 10 supplemental vocabulary words, as in Step One
	30 min.	Activity 5 with Version B of the story
Wednesday	25 min.	Internalization of 10 supplemental vocabulary words, as in Step One
	30 min.	Activity 8
Thursday		Test, emphasizing everything that's in this 2-week period but including material from before
Friday		A game or a cultural activity

Accuracy in Production

In the last few years, Ray and his colleagues have gradually moved away from the teaching of grammar through explanation and drills. They have found and developed much more effective ways of getting students to acquire grammatical features of their new language. These ways involve:

1. comprehensible input *in context* via listening and reading and

2. oral or written production by students *in context.*

These ideas are in harmony with Stephen Krashen and Tracy Terrell's Natural Approach in the way they relate to acquisition and learning (see p. 28 above and Krashen and Terrell, 1983). Ray believes that teaching grammar in traditional ways is "like trying to teach a pig to sing." He can't sing and this annoys the pig. "Studying grammar brings trivial gains from intense study." Ray agrees with Krashen that acquisition occurs through comprehensible input. So he emphasizes input.

Students do four things in TPR Storytelling which directly promote correct grammatical production in context:

*   *Using guide words* — see pages 56-60.

*   *Freewriting* — writing 100 words non-stop in class in 10-15 minutes once each week on a topic given by the teacher. This begins in the second year.

*   *Retelling stories in the 1st-person singular and other persons and tenses.* For example, "The Clothing Store" (on p. 45 above) is originally in the third-person singular (with a little plural) in the simple present tense. It can be retold in the first-person singular (with some first-person plural). Actually, the retelling involves the 3rd-person singular too, because the teller relates the story from the point of view of one of the main characters, Kim or Travis. S/he tells what each character does, and the verb forms are contrasted in a natural way. Since students already know and are able to tell the story, they can focus on the verb forms when they retell it from a different point of view. If a student is telling this story from the point of view of Kim, s/he says things like, "Travis and I are walking ... Travis goes into ... I go to the girls' clothing department ... The clerk gives us ..."

This is perhaps the most effective way to work on a verb form after it has been introduced. (This story and many others can also be retold in the first-person plural. See also no. 3 in Activity 2 on p. 64 and item 6 on pp. 86-87.)

A new verb form is introduced simply by telling the students, for example, that in Spanish to say "I eat" instead of "he or she eats" you just replace the vowel at the end of the verb with an *o*. For verbs that don't fit this pattern (irregular verbs), when they arise the students are told the form. This very simple procedure has proven amazingly successful. The principle is: *When they need it, give it to them.*

TIP: A "quick" student can often be told a new word or form at the point of needing it and will store it immediately for future use. A "slow" student will usually forget it even if s/he needs it. So, in German, for example, when all students know *er hat* for *he has*, if a quick student wants to say "I have," it is worth telling her/him "ich habe," whereas you may be better off waiting than wasting time and cluttering the mind of the slower student with the same information.

Coincidentally, the widely used Natural Approach Spanish college textbook *Dos mundos* utilizes an activity similar to the retelling of stories in different persons and tenses which is called a "narration series" or "serie narrativa"; more of these were added in the 2nd edition because instructors "reported that they were useful for focusing on verb forms and tenses and that students were stimulated by them" (Terrell et al., 1990: *xv*). There are also French (*Deux mondes*, Terrell et al., 1993) and German (*Kontakte*, Terrell et al., 1995) versions of this book.

- *20-second responses on a topic given by the teacher.* The students must respond orally and immediately and keep talking for 20 seconds. The whole class does this in pairs simultaneously. One student in each pair talks for 20 seconds. After 20 seconds, the teacher says, "Stop!" or rings a bell and then says, "Start!" and the partner talks for 20 seconds. After the second partner finishes, the teacher goes around the room telling 5-7 students to share one by one with the class either (1) what they said to their partners or (2) what their partners said to them. This activity (which derives from a segment of the Advanced Placement language test of the Educational Testing Service) is done once a week, and 5 different topics are treated each time. It is used from sometime late in the 1st year on through the 4th year.

For example, the topic might be: "What's your favorite class?" This question provides very little input, so Ray feels it is important for the teacher to provide more input by talking about the topic for a minute or two before providing the topic to the student. The response might begin: "Spanish. When I goes there, I ..." This is where the matter of grammatical correctness comes in. Only in this situation and only for the 1st-person singular present verb form, students are corrected by the teacher in one of two ways, depending on the individual student's ability. If the teacher thinks the student could come up with the correct form on her/his own, the teacher says, "I *goes*. That's not right. Try again." Otherwise, the teacher says, "Listen. This sounds better: 'When I *go* there, ...' "

One very productive way to do 20-second responses is to give students a topic about which they must convince their partner in a 20-second monologue. Then they get another 20 seconds in which to convince their partner of the opposite. For example, "Convince your partner to go see the movie 'Speeding Turtles';" then, "Convince your partner not to see 'Speeding Turtles' but to see 'Divine Inferno' instead."

Ray and his colleagues have had remarkable success in developing accurate production by using contextual activities instead of explaining and drilling grammar. Students are producing language that is more and more grammatically correct, both in writing and in speech at all three levels — 2nd, 3rd and 4th years. Part of this approach to the acquisition of grammatical accuracy comes from Fluency First, which has been developed at City College of the City University of New York (formerly CCNY or City College of New York) largely by Associate Professor of ESL Adele MacGowan-Gilhooly. It is beyond the scope of the book you are reading now to provide a full description of Fluency First; however, it is dealt with thoroughly in MacGowan-Gilhooly's books (see bibliography). Specific activities from Fluency First that are used in TPR Storytelling include freewriting and extensive reading in novels.

Novel reading is used from late in the first year on. The novels must be at a level that the students can understand readily without using a dictionary. Ray and his sister have written a very short novel for late first-year or early second-year Spanish students (Turner and Ray, 1998). Other juvenile novels are available in several languages for the second year and beyond.

In general, both in TPR Storytelling and in the other activities with which Ray and his colleagues complement it, the focus is on meaning rather than form. And yet students get more and more accurate as their fluency develops. They get exposed to so much language in context in a variety of ways — most of them meaningful and engaging — that, without even realizing it, they get a feel more and more for what "sounds right" — the same way that most first language acquisition takes place. (For more on the significance of sounding right and "grammaticality," refer to Burling, 1982; see bibliography.) Very few grammatical aspects of the target language are taught; nearly all are acquired from the stories, their accompanying activities and other supplementary activities.

However, certain grammatical points require special attention that includes explanation in addition to the usual contextual treatment. In the cases of Spanish and French at least, there are two types of grammatical features that need such attention: (1) advanced subjunctive usages and (2) production of items with which interference from students' first language causes problems, such as:

    Amor es maravilloso.   or   *Amour est formidable.*

instead of

    El amor es maravilloso.   or   *L'amour est formidable.*

for   *Love is great.*

or conversely, for native Spanish- and French-speakers learning English:

    The love is great.   instead of   *Love is great.*

for   *El amor es maravilloso.*   or   *L'amour est formidable.*

The learning of verb forms is a major undertaking in many languages. Ray and his colleagues use an unorthodox approach to the acquisition of verb forms, one which is not only unusually easy on learners but also unusually productive in terms of the results it brings. All regular verb forms are displayed on the walls of the classroom, available at all times for every student to see whenever s/he might need one of them — in essays and freewriting as well as in speaking. Despite never being tested on them, students come to use them accurately. See p. 114 regarding verb wall charts.

Another technique that helps with the learning of irregular verb forms is to teach very brief lyrics which can be sung to a simple well-known melody. For example, to help students remember irregular 1st-person singular forms of the Spanish preterite, Ray uses these lyrics to the tune of "Ten Little Indians:"

> Fui, fui, di, vine, tuve, hice, puse, estuve, quise, pude, supe, dije, traje y anduve.

Ray's Stockdale High School colleague Gale Mackey has produced an audio cassette of songs called *Spanish Grammar Songs* (1997) for learning irregular Spanish verb forms and selected others.

In some cases Ray uses a chant rather than a song. He says learning the forms in such songs and chants is not enough to ensure mastery of them for production in context. It is crucial to use them also in mini-stories with guide words (pp. 56-60). This helps students get a feel for the forms, and later they start showing up spontaneously in their speech.

A very effective technique for getting verb forms down is retelling and rewriting stories in different persons and tenses, as mentioned above on p. 65 (Activity 2, item 3) and pp. 72 and below on pp. 86-86 (item 6). If students already can tell a story in the present, they can easily learn to tell it in the past or the future and to tell it from various points of view.

Another approach to the teaching of verb forms involves the use of hand signals or hand TPR for each of the various persons (see pp. 114-115 in Chapter 5, "Acquiring Tenses"). This was the main approach to teaching verb forms for a while in TPR Storytelling, and it still plays a role, but the above-mentioned techniques have become more prominent.

The Third and Fourth Years

In the 3rd year stories reach five or six hundred words in length and are still the centerpiece of the curriculum. When students retell these longer stories, they are not expected to include every detail or to use every new vocabulary item. The four activities mentioned above on pp. 72-74 for the 2nd year continue to be used to develop correct production:

- Guide words are used to focus on certain grammatical features.
- Students are limited to 10 minutes for their 100 words of freewriting.
- They retell stories in various persons and tenses.
- A variety of things may be corrected in 20-second responses in the ways mentioned above.

In addition, in the 3rd year students write journals and do ten pages of outside reading each week as well as silent reading in class. They write a 4-line summary of each page they read. As they read, they make a list of words they don't know and write sentences in which they use these words. They also carry on discussions about "hot topics" that arouse fervent comment by most students. At times students run the discussions, but the teacher provides lots of comprehensible input in every discussion.

They write 200-word essays too, which are corrected and graded on correctness. Correcting is always done "to level," that is, keeping in mind what kind of correction and how much correction will actually help a student to later produce the same type of item correctly. Some errors are not corrected — with the idea that a student can only focus on a limited amount of accuracy at one time. New material and errors that involve material beyond a student's level are never corrected, only things which students are reminded of from earlier in their study of the language. Whenever the teacher thinks the student can come up with the right way, s/he says, "Try this again." Students are encouraged to come in for help before turning their essays in, so that they can score high on them. Perfection is not required for the maximum grade. Ray notes that with this approach "the more advanced students are, the more enthralled they are" with grammatical accuracy.

By the time students have reached 3rd year, they find it very easy to tell stories — even very long stories — from pictures or, often, without. In the 3rd and 4th years the 10 steps in the above procedures on pp. 44-61 for learning to retell a story are boiled down to the following:

1. Internalizing the vocabulary through TPR and mini-stories (with the use of guide words (pp. 56-60) to help es-

tablish certain grammatical features and vocabulary), as in Step One (pp. 44-54)

2. Reading the main story and translating it
3. Telling the main story from pictures (not reading) after preparation with guide words (pp. 56-60)

Their other activities at these levels — described above (3rd year) and below (4th year) — are not based on the main story.

In the 4th year, stories are no longer the core of the curriculum. Students continue to engage in the following activities:

- They are limited to 5 or 6 minutes for their 100 words of freewriting. Sometimes they are told to write on the easiest topic they can think of.
- They retell stories in various persons and tenses.
- They carry on discussions about "hot topics."
- They give 20-second responses.

In addition they do the following:

- Read high-interest novels that deal with issues crucial to the students in the target language, written at a 6th-, 7th- or 8th-grade level.
- Do listening exercises, e.g., watch a movie, take lots of notes. Afterwards they read quotations from characters in the movie and indicate which character said each.
- Write a 200-word essay every week on a topic of interest to all of them given by the teacher; they discuss the topic in class. Some examples of topics are: "A Romantic Date," "Why _____ Is Important" (the student fills in the blank), "Gun Control" and "The Changes that Will Occur in the 21st Century."
- Take 2 minutes to look at a set of 6 pictures that tell a story, then tell the story orally in 2 minutes.

The Daily Class Schedule in the 2nd, 3rd and 4th Years

In the 2nd year about a month is spent on each story and its accompanying activities; the stories are longer than the 1st-year stories. Before daily work on stories is done as described above, the following activities occur each day in the 2nd-, 3rd- and 4th-year Spanish and French classes at Stockdale High School:

Monday	Class discussion
Tuesday	20-second responses
Wednesday	Freewriting
Thursday	A right-or-wrong grammar quiz consisting of 20 items like the following:

> The boy speak a lot.
>
> I speak a lot.
>
> He go to France.

Friday	Reading activities

2nd year:

> Reading an item in a local newspaper that deals with something the students are familiar with, then taking a quiz on it.

3rd & 4th years:

> Taking a quiz on the reading in a novel done as homework, turning in written homework mentioned above (p. 77) based on this reading, class discussion of the reading.

How to Make Sure All Students Perform Adequately

What happens when students are not performing as desired, when students can't tell a story? The failure is nearly always rooted in not having some of the vocabulary down, in not having practiced it enough through TPR and hand TPR. The teacher must take care to check among the less stellar students to make sure they're getting every item. If someone is not getting a particular item, the teacher has the whole class practice it again and checks again. If the less talented students are getting everything, then everybody is.

How Many New Words to Teach in a Story?

Melinda Forward, who teaches French at Springtown High School in Springtown, Texas, recommends that only 8 to 12 new words be taught in a story. Most stories with only 8 to 12 new words in them would be mini-stories.

79

TPR Storytelling Songs

In a special variety of TPR Storytelling, students learn stories in the form of songs. Gale Mackey has produced two audio cassettes (one with an accompanying lyrics and exercise book) with songs in Spanish based on stories in Blaine Ray's first two Spanish books. See *¡Mírame, puedo cantar!: Look, I Can Sing! 1 and 2* (1997a, 1997b) in the bibliography.

TPR Storytelling in Elementary and Middle School

Valeri Marsh (a.k.a. Valeri Waxman-Marsh) and Christine Anderson of the Phoenix, Arizona, area have written excellent Spanish, French and ESL TPR Storytelling text/workbooks for elementary and middle school entitled *¡Cuéntame!* (1994), *¡Cuéntame más!* (1993), *Raconte-moi!* (1994), *Raconte-moi encore!* (1995) and *Tell Me More!* (1998). Carol Gaab, working with Marsh, has written a Spanish K-2 TPRS Curriculum (1998). Thorough teacher's manuals are available for all of these (see bibliography). This group uses oral sounds in addition to or along with hand TPR as the signals for vocabulary items. Gaab, who did the ESL adaptation, recommends that ESL teachers take special care in their choice of gestures and sounds, since there may be some cultural problems with American signs and sounds when teaching speakers of other languages. She avoids translation and instead uses pictures, photos, props and scenarios to get across the meaning of vocabulary items. See "Ways and Means of Getting Across Meaning" on pp. 26-28.

Videos on TPRS for Teachers

Blaine Ray has produced four VHS videocassettes about TPR Storytelling. The *TPR Storytelling Video* (1995) is a basic demonstration of the method. The *New Blaine Ray TPR Storytelling Workshop Video* (2001) features the best segments of a workshop that Ray conducted in Findley, Ohio. The two *¡Mírame, puedo hablar! Mini-Stories Videos* (1998) demonstrate how Ray and Joe Neilson teach all the mini-stories in the book *¡Mírame, puedo hablar! Mini-Stories*.

Other High School Materials

Melinda Forward of the Dallas-Fort Worth area and Shirley Ogle of Río Rancho, New Mexico, have developed other effective TPRS materials for high school French and Spanish. They feature only mini-stories for learning to retell and are unusually thorough and well-organized, giving the teacher step-by-step assistance throughout and abundant student materials. Unlike the other TPRS materials mentioned above, they are organized around thematic units such as shopping and seasons.

What Do Students Achieve with TPR Storytelling?

What kind of results are obtained with TPR Storytelling? All students can tell stories, and they can exchange information in speech. They can comprehend the spoken word to a high degree at the appropriate level. They experience loads of success. Some students are lazy and don't get their points on homework and tests and so get mediocre or lousy grades, but even these develop considerable fluency even in the first year and can tell stories in their new language.

Research done about 25 years ago indicated that as few as 15% of high school students who started studying a foreign language made it to the third year (Lawson: 1971); some 20 years later the figure had risen to 27% (Draper: 1991). In schools using TPR Storytelling throughout their programs, the rate has been consistently over 60% — far above other reported figures.

Ray finds that students who are actually acquiring their new language are generally motivated to continue — that is, students who are expanding the range of what they comprehend aurally and in reading while they become more and more fluent both in speech and in writing. They sign up for the next course and the next (unless other things in their lives get in the way). Students know whether they are actually progressing; receiving a good grade is not the same as actually acquiring the language. Before developing TPR Storytelling, Ray had noticed that generally students who got a high grade without having made real progress lost interest.

Stockdale High School, where Ray teaches, is a public school with about 1,900 students, about 1,100 of whom are enrolled in foreign language classes. Almost no students drop out during the school year. In 1994 and 1995 a total of 69 Stockdale Spanish students passed the Educational Testing Service's Advanced Placement language exam. Over 75% of these were non-native speakers of Spanish. Each year over the four-year span 1995-98, second-year true beginners passed this test. These students did little homework, and none of them lived in a Spanish-speaking country.

Joe Neilson teaches at Salpointe Catholic High School, which has 1,300 students, with about 800 enrolled in Spanish and French classes. When he discovered TPR Storytelling, the Spanish program at Salpointe was using a typical, commonly-used Spanish high school textbook. After some experimentation, Neilson proposed to the school principal that the entire foreign language program switch to TPR Storytelling and he showed him Ray's 1st-year text (1990). The principal looked it over and said, "You can't teach with this! It doesn't have any grammar."

Neilson suggested that they give the National Spanish Examination to all 1st- and 2nd-year Spanish students in the program, then use TPR Storytelling the next year, and then give the NSE again and compare the results. (The NSE is a proficiency and achievement exam which includes grammar and is developed by the American Association of Teachers of Spanish and Portuguese.) The principal agreed to this. The results showed a 45% improvement in the scores of students in 1st-year classes and a 41% increase in scores of 2nd-year students — with the same group of teachers teaching both years. The principal and the whole language staff were delighted with these results, and they have been using TPR Storytelling throughout their program ever since.

Advantages of TPR Storytelling

There are several important advantages to TPR Storytelling. Consider the following list:

1. When students make up their own stories — perhaps the most powerful of all the activities in TPR Storytelling — they are using their imaginations. They are having fun. They get turned on by their own ideas and the ideas of their classmates, as they do when they're just talking among friends in their first language. There appears to be no adaptation (see pp. 159-160 for an explanation of *adaptation*) in this exciting and significant activity.

2. The breadth of what can be dealt with in stories is literally limitless — in topics, form, vocabulary, length, brevity, grammatical structures ... Stories that are told can, in fact, incorporate the entire range of possibilities

of a language, including elements that don't really work well in print, such as, "She made a face like this" — where the accompanying facial expression is part of the telling — or gestures made with a special degree of vehemence, or particular intonations, or emphasis on certain words and phrases, or any kind of special voicing.

3. In most classroom language learning, students rarely produce more than a single sentence at a time. In storytelling there is "connected discourse," as there so often is in real life. The ability to produce in speech one connected idea after another is a skill that must be developed. This is a key element in fluency, one which is often ignored. In TPR Storytelling, as Ray practices it, connected discourse begins to be developed after the first 150 words have been internalized. The development may continue to the point where learners can tell stories that are as long and detailed as stories they can tell in their first language.

4. There seem to be advantages in providing to students a means of producing new vocabulary in context soon after they have demonstrated that they have internalized it.

   a. Ray uses "classical TPR" for the first five weeks, or about the first 150 words. Up through this time there is virtually no production on the part of students. Then he starts in on TPR Storytelling. There is rarely any sign of adaptation, for two reasons: (1) there is continual variation in the activities of the class and (2) the class is generally enthralled with the content, which is often made personally relevant to one or another or all the students (see pp. 50-51 above). In the larger context of the entire gamut of activities used in dealing with a story in TPR Storytelling, there is, for all practical purposes, no adaptation. One means of avoiding adaptation, apparently, is to provide realistic and engaging ways for students to produce new material soon after they have internalized it.

   b. Most students want to talk. Not only do they want to give commands, but they want to say other things and they don't know how to. TPR Storytelling is an excellent way to help students accomplish this from the time of first oral production on.

83

5. TPR Storytelling builds confidence in speaking. Those two students of Ray's who were at the CFLTA workshop performed with amazing ease and almost nonchalance (see pp. 39-40).

6. The results of using storytelling as a major strategy along with TPR are outstanding — perhaps unequaled. The results in regard to spoken production are especially noteworthy. Little if anything compares as an instructional strategy that

   a. develops the ability to speak freely, that is, fluency

   b. encourages students to use their imaginations and creativity

   c. thereby encourages them to take on a large part of the responsibility for learning

   d. builds their confidence in speaking

TPR Storytelling can accomplish very important things that perhaps nothing else can. It is a systematic, entertaining, low-stress way of internalizing pieces of a "cognitive map" of grammatical structures, or of internalizing a "holistic pattern of how the language works," to use a couple of Asher's terms.

Significant New Developments in TPR Storytelling

There have been significant developments in TPR Storytelling (now also known as TPRS) since the first printing of the second edition of this book in 1998. Below is a description of the most important of these developments. There is more detail on these developments in printings of *Fluency Through TPR Storytelling* (Ray and Seely) done in 2001 and later and in the *New Blaine Ray TPR Storytelling Workshop Video* (Ray, 2001).

Three Levels of Stories

In TPR Storytelling there are three levels of stories, which build one upon another. The first is the shortest and the third is the longest. The shortest is the **personalized mini-situation (PMS)**. Three to five PMSs provide the vocabulary for the second level of story—the **mini-story**. In turn, two to four mini-stories provide the vocabulary for the final level—the **main story**, which can range in length from 15 sentences to a hundred or more. Each PMS utilizes three new vocabulary words or phrases. All the vocabulary of a

84

mini-story is taught in PMSs. Generally one PMS is taught per 50-minute daily class. After the PMSs are completed, the corresponding weekly mini-story is taught, with the very same new vocabulary, but in a different context. There is usually one mini-story a week. And after teaching all the PMSs that are based on the mini-stories and teaching two to four mini-stories (all of whose vocabulary comes from a main story), the main story is taught. Through this process students are exposed to each new vocabulary item **aurally some 50 to 100 times**. Initially the items are taught in isolation, but very soon they are put into a variety of meaningful contexts. This is a major key to the success of TPRS.

Vocabulary is taught very well, so that it is nearly impossible to forget it and so that students are able to come up with it when they need it in speech. This does take time but the payoff is far greater than the usual approach of teaching lots of vocabulary in a much shallower way.

To accomplish this thorough ingraining of new vocabulary items, it is essential to focus on getting the students to listen to each item 50 to 100 times in a variety of circumstances that hold their interest. In doing so, care must be taken to **avoid introducing other new words** that the students won't understand and that will distract them from the task at hand. It takes some practice to achieve this. New TPRS teachers generally need to make a special effort to keep focused on this goal and to keep out new words which might distract. Obvious cognates are not a problem, but other words can be. And producing enough occurrences of each new item can be challenging. Careful preparation can help new TPRS teachers do these things well until they become second nature.

The most important part of the entire process of TPR Storytelling is the teaching of personalized mini-situations (PMSs). This is where all the new vocabulary is taught.

The Steps for Teaching a PMS

You have our permission to photocopy this list to use in class:

First of all, make sure you have your main story, the corresponding mini-stories and the corresponding PMSs ready. Make sure they are all **personalized**. They can also be **bizarre** and **exaggerated** (in number and size). Before beginning, put up **all the vocabulary words** for the mini-story (not just for the mini-situation).

1. With each set of three vocabulary items:

Teach the three vocabulary items for the mini-situation with gestures and associations. Mix the items. Ask a maximum of one or two personalized questions for each vocabulary item.

2. Do a closed-eyes comprehension check. When reaction time is very short, assess a barometer student with quick translations of all vocabulary for the mini-story thus far.

3. Choose actors and actresses. Students act out the PMS as you tell it. Tell it; don't memorize the words or read the story. While telling with the performance, ask lots of *who, what, when, where, why, which (one(s)), how, how much, how many* and *how long* questions. Choose the most **bizarre** and **exaggerated** answers to include in the story.

4. The teacher retells the PMS as s/he asks more questions about the details of the story. Students' answers provide new minor details. Teacher moves to the places in the classroom where the actors stood and pantomimes the actions again while s/he retells the PMS.

(Optional: 4z. The whole class acts out the mini-situation as the teacher retells.)

5. Students retell to each other in pairs; 15- or 30-second limit per student.

6. Teach "from perspective," that is, from a different perspective or point of view than was used in the first telling. Normally the first telling is mostly or entirely in the third-person narrative form, e.g., *Angie runs to the elephant and kisses him on the trunk. Then she gives him her suitcase....* Now **the storyteller is the main character** and tells the story in the first person.

   a. If possible, show the class how to do this in their first language. From Angie's point of view the story goes: *I run to the elephant and kiss him on the trunk. Then I give him my suitcase....* (After you've done this with a few stories, you won't have to do it in the students' first language any more.)

   b. Before they tell from perspective, students must be prepared to make the necessary changes. These are called **guide words** (this is a new usage for this

86

term). Write these out on the overhead or board, e.g.:

runs	I run
kisses	I kiss
gives	I give
her	my

Then point out and pronounce the differences for the students as necessary.

7. Students retell the PMS "from perspective."

8. (optional) Students retell without guide words or vocabulary words.

The Steps for Teaching a Mini-Story

After teaching all the PMSs in which the students have pretty much acquired the new vocabulary that will appear in the corresponding mini-story (10 to 15 items), you teach that mini-story. You use the same procedures that you use for the mini-stories except that you omit the first two steps, since there is no new vocabulary. In steps 5 and 7 (and 8) the time limit for students to retell in pairs may be a little longer than it is for PMSs. It is kept brief, in any event, to keep everyone on task.

Chapter 5:
Acquiring Tenses through TPR

Verb tenses and persons can be acquired in various ways that involve TPR, for example, through:

- Natural Action Dialogs
- TPR Storytelling
- Hand TPR
- Action Series
- Jody Klopp's Tense-Acquisition Exercises
- Berty Segal Cook's Four Levels of Questions
- TPR Treatment of Paul Pimsleur's "Horizontal" Approach to Verb Forms

No matter what way or ways are used to acquire tenses in the various persons, for some languages there is a pertinent question worth considering before ever beginning to use TPR. With TPR we make a transition from an imperative, or some other form of request, to tenses and persons. The most useful and common tense, perhaps universally, is a present tense. If there is more than one form of request in the target language, it is likely to be easier to make the transition to the present tense with one of the request forms than with another (or others). For most teachers of Spanish, French, German, Italian, Portuguese and many other languages, this is a radically different approach from the usual. The traditional and most-used way of learning the forms of the persons of the present is based on the infinitive. Like many applied linguists, we find it far more effective to start with the base form of the present tense if such a form is a singular request form in the target language. For a few commonly studied languages, consider the following:

- English: The base form is the dictionary form, which is conveniently the same as the imperative — *talk*.

- Spanish: The base form of the present tense is almost without exception the 3rd-person singular, which is identical to the *tú* affirmative — *habla, come*. Another choice for making requests is the *usted* form of the present tense, which is used for polite requests, usually with the word *usted* included. This form is nearly always identical to the *tú* affirmative imperative with two added advantages: (1) having objective and reflexive pronouns precede it (*se quita, lo come*), as they do generally in the tenses, rather than being attached to the end in the case of the affirmative imperative (*quítate, cómelo*) and (2) avoiding irregular imperatives such as *ven* and *pon*.

- French: Conveniently, the *tu* imperative form is pronounced the same as most singular forms of the present tense.

- German: In most cases the *du* imperative is the basic form to which endings are added to make present tense forms, although there are many irregularities.

- Italian: Generally the short *tu* imperative is identical to either the 1st- or the 3rd-person singular of the present tense. While this favors the acquisition of the forms of the present tense, the *Lei* imperative has the advantage of taking object pronouns before the verb, where they belong when used with tenses.

- Japanese: Fortunately there are no distinctions according to person. The most generally acceptable choice is the *-te kudasai* form used along with the simple *-te* form. In *Iki Iki Nihongo: Live Action Japanese*

(Fukuda et al., 1994) for variety we also used the
-*mashō* form.

* Chinese: No problem. There is only one form of every
verb.

Natural Action Dialogs

We suggest you consult pp. 28-32, "Natural Action Dialogs," for
further information about using material like that provided in
this section. Note that it is often useful to employ a TPR dictation
(see pp. 139-141) in connection with student oral/aural practice of
natural action dialogs and that in some circumstances doing
some work on pronunciation is worthwhile.

Present Continuous (Present Progressive)

Base this activity on an action series which is currently familiar to your students. Start with the pantomime game, as follows.
Pantomime, without props, one of the actions of an action series,
asking the students at the same time, "What am I doing?" They
will probably answer with the appropriate line from the series, in
the now *inappropriate* (in English) imperative form. For example,
if you are washing your hands, and you ask them "What am I doing?", they will probably respond with "wash your hands."
Encourage them, saying, "That's right, I'm *washing* my hands."
Repeat this with every action in the series. After they've heard
your "new" version several times, write this new verb form on the
board and explain that you're no longer giving instructions, as
you were doing before (imperative form), but are now talking
about an action that is happening right now, at the same time
they're talking. Demonstrate other actions in the same way, quite
a few more times, prompting them to use the new -*ing* forms of
the verbs.

(Note: If the students respond correctly, with the correct form of
the present continuous (in many languages this would be the simple present) the very first time you present this, it means that
they are already familiar with this verb tense, its formation, and
its use and meaning. They may or may not need to go ahead and
practice it further. If, however, the present continuous is indeed

91

new to them or they haven't sufficiently acquired it to be able to respond appropriately to your initial question as suggested above, they will need to go through this exercise many times with many different action series in order to get enough exposure and practice to actually acquire it.)

Then ask members of the class to do certain actions, and ask the class what they're doing. Better yet, ask them to do *any* action from the lesson — this is much more interesting: "Luis, show us a different action from the same lesson: no, don't say anything, just do one action. Look, everybody, look at Luis. What is he doing?" Point out that the verb *to be* is used here and that it changes depending on the person talked about (*you're, I'm, he's, she's, we're, they're*; depending on the abilities and level of the class and on whether they are already using these pronoun-verb combinations in another context, these might have to be dealt with one at a time.)

If the class is capable of handling a little more at this time, along with the present continuous (see no. 2 above on p. 31), this is an especially good exercise for actions involving ***possessive adjectives***:

> "Luis, wash your hands. What's *he* doing?"
> "He's washing *his* hands."
>
> "Anne, wash your hands. What's *she* doing?"
> "She's washing *her* hands."
>
> "Look, everybody, what am *I* doing?"
> "You're washing *your* hands."

This is a very real and natural way to practice these possessives.

After the class has practiced as a group enough so that many members are able to produce accurate oral responses in the various persons, you may move on.

Small group practice. Arrange the students in groups of 4 or 5 (at least one female and one male in each group so both feminine and masculine forms will be practiced). Have them tell each other which action to do and then ask each other what I/you/he/she/we/ they are doing:

Roberto:	Mei Ling, light the candle.
Marie:	Sara, what is Mei Ling doing?
Sara:	She's lighting the candle.

Mei Ling:	Sara and Roberto, blow out the match.
Marie:	Paolo, what are they doing?
Paolo:	They're blowing out the match.

(based on "Candle" in Romijn and Seely: 1988: 2)

Notice that this is also an excellent contrast of the two forms (imperative/basic form vs. present continuous/-*ing* form). This is one of the most unique aspects of this exercise. The present continuous tense is usually considered to be acquired when the student begins to utter it with the correct form but without regard to the correct context. If the student accurately produces the present continuous tense but uses it in a context where another tense is needed instead, then how can we say that the tense is acquired? Doesn't acquisition entail correct and appropriate *usage and context* in addition to correct *formation*? As mentioned on pages 28-30 in Chapter 2, the two are usually taught separately and even at different levels of fluency *if usage and meaning are addressed at all*. The approach suggested in this chapter is a unique method of helping students to acquire the usage *along with* the form of each tense. Here several different tenses are contrasted by drilling them together, always in a natural and realistic context, to demonstrate the differences in meaning. Where most materials have a separate unit for each tense, this approach suggests practicing *several* tenses every day. Furthermore, each tense, once introduced, is practiced regularly *throughout the course.*

Practice of negative forms. Here are the first lines of "Chewing Gum" in Romijn and Seely (1988: 6):

1. Go to the store.

2. Buy a pack of gum.

3. Open the pack.

4. Take out a piece of gum.

The dialogs that follow are based on the above lines. Students must be very familiar with the action series on which this model of dialog is based. It's great fun to go through a whole series doing this with each step:

Teacher:	Go to the store.
Students:	(physical response, in pantomime or real)
Teacher:	Don't go to the bathroom!
Students:	(You'll have to prompt them at first.)
	I'm *not* going to the bathroom!
Teacher:	Where *are* you going?
Students:	I'm going to the store.
Teacher:	(optional) Oh, excuse me!

Teacher:	Buy a pack of gum.
Students:	(physical response, in pantomime or real)
Teacher:	Don't buy candy!
Students:	I'm *not* buying candy!
Teacher:	What *are* you buying?
Students:	I'm buying a pack of gum.
Teacher:	(optional) Oh, excuse me!

Teacher:	Take out a piece of gum.
Students:	(physical response, in pantomime or real)
Teacher:	Don't take out three pieces!
Students:	I'm *not* taking out three pieces!
Teacher:	How many *are* you taking out?
Students:	I'm taking out one (piece).
Teacher:	(optional) Oh, excuse me!

Here is the basic model for this natural action dialog:

Teacher: (command from familiar action series)

Students: (physical response, in pantomime or real)

Teacher: Don't _____ !

Students: I'm *not* _____-ing _____ !

Teacher: Wh-___ *are* you _____-ing?

Students: I'm _____-ing _____ .

Teacher: (optional) Oh, excuse me!

The whole class can do this together, or it may be done with individual students. Notice that this dialog contrasts the formation, use and meaning of:

1. the **affirmative** and **negative** forms of the **imperative** and

2. the **affirmative, negative** and **interrogative** forms of the **present continuous**.

This can be a lot of fun, with silly instructions such as "Don't stick it (the piece of gum) in your ear!" Notice that these dialogs expose students to **Wh- questions** along with the **present continuous**.

Simple Past

Have several people each perform a different step of a familiar action series; or, when this is not appropriate, have 3 or 4 different people each perform a section of the series. Then ask, "Who _____-ed?" about each action. For example:

Who lit the candle?   Anna (did).
Who blew it out?   Boris (did).

The whole class answers *en masse*, using only names, thereby hearing, understanding and responding even to past forms which are brand new to them. If the students have trouble remembering each other's names, which might be the case in some mixed ESL classes or in classes that meet infrequently, it helps to mention the names several times, to write them on the board or to limit the number of people who are doing the actions.

At the same time that the students' names are being written on the board, we have found it useful to also write the past forms of the verbs being used. We do this for two reasons. First, it shows the spelling of the new words, so that the students begin to get accustomed to the differences and similarities between the way the words are pronounced and the way they are spelled. Secondly, it emphasizes the fact that these are actually new and different forms of the verb. In fact, to demonstrate this even more clearly, we usually list not only the simple past forms on the board, but also the basic forms right next to them:

Basic Forms	Past Forms
put	put
take out	took out
tear	tore
light	lit
blow	blew
throw	threw
look	looked
smell	smelled
feel	felt

(based on "Candle" in Romijn and Seely: 1988: 2)

This not only emphasizes the association between words such as *take* and *took,* but also clears up confusion, before it develops, around such pairs as *put* and *put* or *read* [reed] and *read* [red]. Such lists may also be used to drill pronunciation, especially of the very challenging regular ending *-ed*. When there are only two or three examples of *-ed*, as in the list above, the individual forms can be drilled and contrasted with the present forms, simply pointing out that in these words the letter *e* is silent. Some action series, however, have many regular verbs:

Basic Forms	Past Forms
heat	heated
pick	picked
open	opened
pour	poured
add	added
stir	stirred
put	put
cover	covered
turn	turned

wait	waited
take off	took off
check	checked

(based on "Soup For Lunch" in Romijn and Seely: 1988: 31)

In such cases, generalizations may be pointed out during the pronunciation practice about when the *e* is silent and when it is pronounced (after final *d* or *t.*)

We generally do not describe the rule about when the final *d* is pronounced [t] and when it is pronounced [d]. It is our experience that describing this rule is not helpful. This is a phonological rule that will or will not be acquired naturally when the student has enough experience with the language.

In any event, the important thing is that these verb forms and spelling and pronunciation rules are being taught strictly in the context of actions that are really taking place in your classroom. They will be reinforced and practiced again at the end of the lesson if the TPR Dictation is used, as described on pp. 139-141 of Chapter 7.

Note also that **two-part verbs** such as *take off* and *take out* are being introduced to the students in these lessons without fanfare, in a natural and contextual way. We find this to be much more helpful and interesting to the students than the usual long lists of **two-part verbs or "idioms"** presented out of context.

When the students have become familiar with the appropriate past form of each verb in the series, they can ask the same *Who _____-ed?* questions of each other in small groups. (If this is done in the following class session, the above steps should be repeated first.) It is useful to do this same exercise with many different action series over a period of many class sessions or even throughout the entire semester. This is fun and it gets easier the more the students get used to it.

To practice *negative past* and contrast it with the affirmative, use "tricky questions:"

> T: Why did (Thi) (break the chair)?
>
> S: She *didn't* (break the chair).

T: What did she (break)?

S: She (*broke* the plate).

(from "A Broken Plate" in Romijn and Seely, 1988: 36)

This is even more fun; what especially contributes to the fun is that the intonation of the second line is one of denial and incredulity, as if the first question were absurd.

TIPS:

• This is a very useful procedure that can be used to practice the negative of any tense and contrast it with the affirmative; any series that a class is already familiar with can be used. An example with the present continuous is given above on pp. 94-95.

• To indicate time for the natural action dialogs above and below — past, present or future — you can write on the board or the overhead such things as *3 p.m., 2002* or *last night*. This can be useful in many other situations as well.

Future with Going to *or* Will

Assign a different person to each step of the series and then discuss who's going to do what *before you let anyone actually perform any of the actions*:

Cleo, will you please pick up your pencil and give it to Thi?

OK, good, but not yet, Cleo, wait a minute.

Thi, when Cleo gives you her pencil, will you feel it with your thumb?

OK, but not yet, wait.

Then Sara, you can borrow my pencil sharpener (but not yet) and then give it to Boris.

Boris will stick the pencil in the hole. OK, Boris?

But don't sharpen it. Give it to Roberto.

And Roberto, you sharpen it, OK?

Now wait a minute, does everybody remember?
(The teacher has students answer the following questions *en masse* or individually or alternating between the whole group and individuals:)

Who's going to pick up her pencil? (Cleo is.)

Who's going to feel it with her thumb? (Thi is.)

Who's going to borrow my pencil sharpener? (Sara is.)

Who's going to stick the pencil in the hole? (Boris is.)

Who's going to sharpen the pencil? (Roberto is.)

> (from "Sharpening Your Pencil" in Romijn and Seely, 1988: 9)

To practice *short answers*:

> Is Boris going to sharpen the pencil? (No, he's not.)
>
> Is Cleo going to pick up her pencil? (Yes, she is.)

When the students are ready to begin forming sentences with this tense themselves (this would probably be after the above questions have been practiced with several, or even many, other series):

> What's Cleo going to pick up?
>
> (She's going to pick up her pencil.)
>
> What's Thi going to feel it with?
>
> (She's going to feel it with her thumb.)
>
> Who's Sara going to borrow the sharpener from?
>
> Where is Boris going to stick the pencil?
>
> What's Roberto going to do?

All of these questions can be practiced in pairs when the students are ready to form questions themselves. They can also be dictated (in a TPR dictation; see pp. 139-141) before or after the pair practice, *but always before the actual action so that the context will remain real.* Then be sure to really have them perform the actions again to make all the predictions of the exercise come true (again to make the context real).

Contrasting the past and future tenses. After having worked on the future with an action series in one or more natural action dialogs, you may wish to give the same series a similar treatment with the past tense. You have talked about the actions in the future and the actions have consequently been performed; now they can be described in the past. This could be done either immediately or during the next class session. In this way the contrast between these two tenses can be pointed out and emphasized.

Simple Present
(in contrast with *present continuous* or *present progressive*)

This tense has been placed *after* the **past** and **future tenses** in this section because it involves a much more abstract concept in English than either of these two tenses. The *meanings* of both the **future** and **past tenses** are very easy to demonstrate in a contextual way with TPR, while the **simple present** does not lend itself so readily to contextual demonstration. Furthermore, it is our experience that the *formation* of the **simple present** is *also* much more complicated than the forms of either the **future** or the **simple past.** This formation includes the difficult-to-hear final -*s* in the third-person singular (a rule for which a lot of time can be wasted with beginning students who are not going to be ready to acquire it for many months) and with its complex formation of the **interrogative form** with *do* and *does.* We have found that the **interrogative form of the simple present** is easier to learn *after* exposure to the *similar* **interrogative form of the simple past** with *did.* This is because the **simple past** involves the same formulation for all persons, while the **simple present** has all the aforementioned differences in the third-person singular (*does* instead of *do,* final -*s*) — just that much more for the students to try to keep track of while they are trying to correctly place the challenging English auxiliary in their questions.

For this natural action dialog, it is assumed that the class is already producing the **present continuous** with some facility. For the **simple present** in *English* you probably *don't* want to use a single action series as the basis for your natural action dialog, because if you did the dialog would not be natural (although in most languages it would be fine). Instead you may choose any actions which are appropriate that you know the students are familiar with, from several action series or any other source.

It is useful to put in a prominent position props and illustrations that will serve as cues for the natural action dialog, e.g., an ice cream cone (plastic or illustration), a movie theater (illustration), a mail box (box or illustration), a television set (real, box or illustration), an egg (plastic). Then tell the whole class to perform familiar commands related to the props and illustrations:

- Eat some ice cream.
- Go to the movies.
- Write a letter.
- Watch T.V.
- Scramble an egg.

Just after each action is completed, you say, for example:

- I eat ice cream every day.
- I often go to the movies.
- I don't write many letters.
- I watch T.V. every night.
- I scramble an egg every morning.

And you mention a few times as this process is going on that we use this form when we talk about things that we do with some frequency, not when we talk about something we're doing right now as we're speaking. If you believe your class is not ready to deal with *don't*, then leave it out for now (although it has been our experience that students who have been introduced to the word *don't* through TPR in the **imperative form** do not tend to have the usual problematic reaction to it when it comes up in the present tense — they are already familiar with it and usually take it in stride, recognizing it as a negative marker.) To get the dialog going, suggest that an individual student do any one of the actions that the whole group just did.

Kareem: (Does action as above.)

Teacher: What are you doing?

Kareem: I'm eating ice cream.

Teacher: Do you eat ice cream every day?

Kareem: Yeah, I eat it every day.
          (*or*: No, I don't eat it every day.)

For some groups it would be sufficient to ask only the question with *every day*. For others you may include questions with *how often*:

Inez: (Does action without stopping until she has answered the first question. In some cases, she must do it slowly for proper timing.)

Teacher: What are you doing?

Inez: I'm going into the theater.

Teacher: How often do you go to the movies?

Inez: I go about once a month.

You may introduce more expressions of frequency, although for many groups the above would be sufficient to begin with. Some others: *always, never, seldom, frequently, now and then, occasionally, almost always, very seldom, hardly ever*.

After several members of the class have become fairly proficient in answering the teacher's questions about these actions, have them split into small groups of 2 to 5 and practice the same natural action dialog. They should actually do or mime the actions as they practice.

The other persons — she, he, we, they — may be practiced in a similar way.

TIP: Pay attention to whether or not the students seem to actually perceive the difference in meaning and usage between these two present tenses. If you are not sure that they do, you can check by asking about an activity, such

(This tip continues on the next page.)

---

as *chewing gum* or *taking notes* that some, but not all, of the students in class are doing at the moment. Ask one student whether or not she *is doing* that activity, and then whether or not she ever *does* it, and ask another student the same two questions but in a different order:

Teacher: Natalia, are you chewing gum?
(*Don't* help her by adding the words *right now.*)

Natalia: No.

Teacher: Do you chew gum?
(*Don't* help her by including the word *ever.*)

Natalia: Yes.

Correct answers can be monitored since you can probably see whether or not Natalia is chewing gum, and she will realize herself that the second question is different, or why would you be asking it right after the first? Then change the order of the two questions randomly for other students in order to coax them into paying attention to which form you are using. You will probably catch quite a few of them giving incorrect responses. Explaining at that point what is wrong with their answers will be quite effective. Continue to ask similar questions until everyone responds appropriately.

Present Perfect

Since the uses of the **present perfect** in the following natural action dialogs occur in the context of the temporal concepts *yet*, *not yet*, *already* and *so far*, one or more action series, in which events occur in a fixed order, provide an ideal basis for them.

1. **Negative with *yet***

    Ask a student to read a certain step of the series, for example line 6 from "Using a Pay Phone" (Romijn and Seely, 1988: 30):

    Student: Stick the change in the slot.

Teacher: Wait a minute! (*or*: I can't!)
Student: What's the matter? (*or*: Why not?)
(You will have to prompt the student with this the first few times)
Teacher: I *haven't taken* the change out yet.*
Student: Well, take it out.
(Again, student will need prompting for this.)

As with the **simple past** on pp. 95-96, when this additional verb form, the **past participle**, is introduced with these dialogs, it is wise to write the forms of the verbs in question on the board or the overhead *with their other two forms:*

Basic Form	**Past Form**	**Past Participle**
take	took	taken

*NOTE: In **Spanish** the **present tense** is most commonly used in the above situation, so this would be a natural action dialog involving the present tense in the same context. This would be useful for English-speaking students of Spanish. In Spanish this line would normally be: *Todavía no saco el suelto*. Teachers of Spanish and other languages will want to pay attention to what verb tenses are used in the languages they are teaching in this and the other contexts presented here for the present perfect in English.)

Repeat this format with several different steps of the series and a different student for each one. This is not as natural as some of the other action dialogs presented in this section, because of the prompting necessary. Even though it's a little awkward, it is a very good introduction to the **present perfect tense** and provides good comprehensible input of this tense.

After doing several dialogs of the same form — each with content that is based on a different step of the series — have the students try doing some with each other, actually performing the actions. Or, if they don't seem ready for that yet, dictate a few of the dialogs for them (see "TPR Dictation," pp. 139-141), pointing out before or during the dictation how the tense is formed. Then have some students write it on the board so that you can correct what's on the board and the students can correct their papers themselves. Now they have a written dialog (or several) which they can use for pair practice.

2. *Affirmative* with *already*. Pantomime an action from the series and then have a student read that imperative to you as you finish up your pantomime:

> Teacher: (Pantomimes the action.)
> Student: Stick the change in the slot.
> Teacher: I've *already* stuck the change in the slot.
> Student: Oh, excuse me!
> (The student will need prompting.)

This is a little awkward like the previous dialog, or even more so, since it is so short. But again, it provides excellent input of a very typical use of this tense. Follow the same procedure described for the previous dialog.

To expand this dialog and give it a real life application, ask students to think of a situation at their jobs or in their homes where someone might ask them to do something which they've already done. Then provide them with the past participle of the verbs they use in their examples and have them perform the dialogs with you or another student. For example:

> My boss: Sweep the large office.
> Me: I've *already swept* the large office.
> (*or*: I've already swept it.)
> My boss: Oh, great.

3. *Interrogative* with *yet*

Have a student do the entire series again but stop him/her after the first two steps, then ask what he's done so far.

Teacher: Juan, go into the phone booth.
Juan: (action)
Teacher: Now check the coin return.

(PLEASE NOTE: The preceding line in *Live Action English* is omitted in some versions of the book in other languages, since in some countries there is no coin return to check.)

Juan: (action)
Teacher: Have you gone into the phone booth yet?
Juan: Yes, I have.
Teacher: Have you checked the coin return?
Juan: Yes, I have.
Teacher: Have you picked up the receiver yet?
Juan: No, not yet.
Teacher: Have you taken out the correct change?
Juan: No, I haven't.
(etc.)

You can now continue through the series with Juan, again stopping after a few steps and asking these questions again.

You can also ask *wh-* questions with *so far*:

What have you done so far?

and:

Is there anything you haven't done yet?

Students can then do this natural action dialog in pairs or small groups if you feel they're ready to. Otherwise, you can do a TPR dictation that will help them comprehend it more fully and provide them with a script to practice with (see pp. 139-141).

Future Tenses with If ... will
(based on "Using a Pay Phone," Romijn and Seely, 1988: 30)

First the teacher says to a student:

Adriana, dial the number.

Wait a minute.

If your friend answers, talk to him.

But if it's busy, whistle a tune.

O.K., go ahead.

Then, after the teacher gives the above instructions but before the student performs the action, the teacher says to another student or the whole class:

> T: What'*ll* she *do* first?
>
> S: She'*ll dial* the number.
> (Accept a response without '*ll* or
> prompt S to use '*ll*, which is new.)
>
> T: What'*ll* she *do* if her friend answers?
>
> S: She'*ll talk* to him.
>
> T: What'*ll* she *do* if it's busy?
>
> S: She'*ll whistle* a tune.

After doing this with one student, the teacher does it with the whole class. Then the students practice this natural action dialog in pairs or small groups. When they have finished, the teacher again tells Adriana to check the coin return. This time she does it and makes a ringing sound or a sound of a busy signal; then she either talks to her friend or whistles a tune.

This lesson can, of course, be done with the ***going to* future** in English just as well as with the ***will* future**.

The previous lesson leads right into a very similar lesson on the ***past "unreal" conditional***. The following natural action dialog can follow immediately the one above in the same class session, or it may be done in the next session or later. If it is done on a different day, the action should be performed again before the teacher says to a student:

> T: What did she do?
>
> S: She whistled a tune.
>
> T: Why didn't she talk to her friend?
>
> S: Because it was busy.

> T: What *would she have done if* her friend *had answered?*
>
> S: She *would have talked* to him.
> (Accept a response without *would have* or prompt S to use *would have* + past participle, which is new.)

or:

> T: What did she do?
>
> S: She talked to her friend.
>
> T: Why did she talk to her friend?
>
> S: Because her friend answered the phone.
>
> T: What *would she have done if* her friend *hadn't answered* the phone?
>
> S: She *would have* whistled a tune.

As with the future tense, after doing this with one student, the teacher does it with the whole class. Then the students practice it in pairs or small groups.

As always, all of these exercises can be followed by dictations (see "TPR Dictation," pp. 139-141) and pronunciation practice.

Below (pp. 110-111) is another treatment of the past "unreal" conditional, one which does not require the use of an action series.

Review of Simple Past, Future With If ... will
Introduction of Past "Unreal" Conditional:
If ... would have
(a High Intermediate Lesson)

1. **Context**
   a. Use any life-skills situation, or vocabulary you think they need or is tricky for some reason, e.g., *taste, try on, fit, cost, lend / borrow, buy / sell, tell / say, ask.*

   b. Form: Set it up as a conditional situation with two or three possible outcomes, e.g.:
      to Student 1:   Ask Student 2 if he'll lend you
                       some money.

to Student 2:   Ask her how much she wants to borrow.

If she wants less than $1, lend it to her.

If she wants between one and ten dollars, tell her to wait until later today.

If she wants more than $10, refuse.

2. **Check comprehension** of words *borrow / lend* and *refuse* by asking if students understand. If they're not sure, explain, demonstrate and practice with TPR commands. The distinction between *borrow* and *lend* may be unclear for speakers of certain languages.

3. **Review of future tense**

Ask whole group:

T: What's Student 1 going to ask Student 2?

S: She's going to ask if he'll lend her some money.

T: What's Student 2 going to ask Student 1?

S: He's going to ask how much she wants to borrow.

T: What will he do if she wants 25 cents?

S: He'll lend it to her.   (less than $1)

T: What will he do if she wants 5 dollars?

S: He'll tell her to wait until later.   ($1 to $10)

T: What will he do if she wants $35?

S: He'll refuse.   (more than $10)

Procedures:
1. Teacher asks whole group.
2. Students ask each other (whole group listening).
3. Pair practice.
4. Dictation and corrections (see pp. 139-141).
5. Pronunciation practice of *gonna* and *what'll'e do?*
6. Introduce reduced form of question (without *will he do*), e.g.: *What if she wants more than $10?*
7. Introduce or review use of comma after but not before *if*-clause.
8. Pair practice of dictation.

---

4. **Action**. Students 1 and 2 actually perform as planned.

5. **Review Simple Past tense**

Ask: "What did S1 ask?"
"What did S2 ask?"
"How much did S1 want?"
"Did S2 lend it to her?"
"Why did he ...?"
"Why *didn't* he ...?"   (etc.)

Procedures:
1. Teacher — whole group
2. Student — student (teacher monitored)
3. Pair practice
4. Dictation and corrections
5. Pronunciation practice, especially of *"What'd'e ...?"*
6. Pair practice

---

6. **Introduce past "unreal" conditional**

Ask: "What would S2 have done if ...?"
"Would he have ... if ...?"

Procedures:

1. Teacher — whole group. If this is new and/or difficult, you may not go any further than just having them respond to these questions as well as they can (only enough to assess comprehension).
2. If comprehension is easy and many are able to even formulate an answer (with prompting from teacher) with correct form, give dictation, of statement form only (no questions), on board, and point out form.
3. If this goes easily, dictate *questions* and answers, then correct, then do pair practice.
4. If students are quite fluent and capable of using these forms correctly (advanced students), have them practice among themselves with teacher monitoring, and then in pairs, *before* dictation.

Below are two examples of a **natural action dialog in Japanese**. An English translation is given afterwards. In this case what is being internalized and practiced is a form of expression that is odd to most non-Japanese. Thus it serves as a good example of what students of a new language often face. The literal translation given below, *became able to*, shows how strange this is from a non-Japanese perspective. Of course, to speakers of Japanese it is totally normal.

Potential verb form: *yō ni naru* / *-n desu*. This activity is called "Chotto dekinai" ("I Can't Do It") (from Noguchi, 1995: 16-17; slightly revised from Fukuda et al., 1994: *xxxix* and *xlvi*). After hearing the first request in a series, the student must use the negative of the potential verb form and then tell why s/he cannot perform the action. Making these "excuses" also gives students the opportunity to practice *-n desu*. It is the responsibility of the other students to come up with various forms of "help" until the student is able to perform the action so that the sequence can be continued.

Example (using "Sōji" ("Cleaning House") in Fukuda et al., 1994: 106-107):

Teacher: (to Student A) Nagashi ni kurenzā o fu-rikakete kudasai.

Student A: Kurenzā ga nakunarimashita no de, fu-rikakerarenai n desu.

Student B: Watashi no kurenzā wa sukoshi nokotte imasu kara, dōzo tsukatte kudasai. (performs action of giving)

Student A: Dōmo arigatō. (performs action of apply-ing cleanser)

Students: A-san wa kurenzā o furikakerareru yō ni narimashita.

Translation of the above natural action dialog:

Teacher: (to Student A) Shake some cleanser into the sink.

Student A: I can't shake any cleanser, because the cleanser has run out.

Student B: I have a little cleanser left, so please use mine. (performs action of giving)

Student A: Thank you. (performs action of applying cleanser)

Students: Mr. A became able to shake the cleanser.

The example continues:

Teacher: (to Student B) Daidokoro no yuka o hōki de haite kudasai.

Student B: Hakenai desu. Koshi ga itai n desu.

Student C: Massāji shite agemashō ka. (performs ac-tion)

Student B: Itakunaku narimashita. Arigatō. (performs sweeping action)

Students: B-san wa yuka o hōki de hakeru yō ni narimashita. (etc.)

Translation of the above natural action dialog:

Teacher: (to Student B) Please sweep the kitchen floor with a broom.

Student B: I can't sweep it, because my back hurts.

Student C: Shall I massage it for you? (performs action)

Student B: It doesn't hurt any more. Thanks. (performs sweeping action)

Students: Mr. B became able to sweep the floor. (etc.)

For lower-level students, the *-ru koto ga dekinai* pattern may be practiced instead of the potential verb forms.

TPR Storytelling

The medium of storytelling allows for great variety and flexibility. Through consistent use of TPR Storytelling techniques with, for example, the simple past tense, students really start getting it. They start "picking up" the regularities and the irregularities while they're concentrating on *getting the meaning* of the story and on *conveying the meaning* to others when they tell the story. Part of the meaning is the "pastness." In general stories are told mainly in the third-person singular and plural of the simple present or the simple past. In TPR Storytelling students relate the various events of a story after they have acquired the vocabulary through TPR and hand TPR (see pp. 44-49). In Step 4 of the procedures for students to learn to tell a story (pp. 58-62), "guide words" are useful for the acquisition of verb forms, especially irregular ones. Later on, after they are thoroughly familiar with the story and have done a variety of activities that revolve around the vocabulary of the story, they are given a single form, the first-person singular. This is done just by telling them, "To say 'I do something,' you change the verb like this;" then a few examples are given orally (see p. 75). Then they retell the same story in a different tense or from a different point of view, for example, they take the part of one of the characters in the story and tell it from his/her point of view. This is remarkably effective. For example, here is a "mini-story":

Fernando kissed Monique. She slapped him.

Here is the same story in the present:

Fernando kisses Monique. She slaps him.

Here is the original story told from Fernando's point of view:

I kissed Monique. She slapped me.

And from Monique's point of view:

Fernando kissed me. I slapped him.

This is done with very long stories as well. As students retell numerous stories in this fashion, they acquire the tenses in the various persons. For more on this, see Chapter 4, "TPR Storytelling," especially pp. 75-76.

Most TPR Storytelling practitioners also use wall charts that show verb forms. The charts stay on the walls for students to find or check the form they need whenever they like, even during most tests. No matter what approach is used — TPR, TPRS or whatever — wall charts generally help students master verb forms (see p. 79). Teachers can make their own, or at least for Spanish and French, they can buy them. Pam Katz, who teaches at Halton High School in Forth Worth, Texas, and her colleague Laurie Nesrala, in the San Dieguito High School District in Encinitas, California, have a Spanish one called *The Verb Wall* (date unknown). Shirley Ogle has one called *The Spanish Verb Timeline* (1997). Her colleague Melinda Forward has a French one available called *The French Verb Timeline* (1997).

Hand TPR

Another approach to the teaching of verb forms involves the use of hand signals or hand TPR (see pp. 41 and 44-49) for each of the various persons. This was developed by Blaine Ray and was used for a time in TPR Storytelling to facilitate the acquisition of verb forms.

- For *I* you touch your chest with your forefinger.
- For *you* singular, you point straight out in front away from your body.
- For formal *you* singular, you move your open hand, palm up, directly out in front away from the body as if offering something to someone in respect; simultaneously you bow your head slightly in respect.
- For *she* you touch either jaw with your index finger.

- For *he* you touch either temple with your index finger.

- For *we* you touch each side of your chest one after the other.

- For formal *you* plural, you do the same as for formal *you* singular, but you use both hands, one beside the other.

- For the other plurals, *you* and *they*, you use the same sign as for the singular, except that you use two fingers, the index and the middle.

In the same way hand TPR can be used to distinguish tenses. Common hand signals are:

- Past tense: Point over your shoulder, behind you.

- Present tense (happening now): Point down at the ground.

- Future tense: Point directly forward.

Of course, all of the above are arbitrary signs, and others could be used in place of any of them. After learning at least two or three of the signs for persons in the same way that they learn hand signs for vocabulary (see pp. 44-49), students use the appropriate one as a physical response when the teacher says, for example, "We go to the house" (Spanish: "Vamos a la casa." French: "Nous allons a la maison." This technique is particularly useful for languages that have many verb forms, like Spanish and French.) When students can give physical responses without hesitation, they have internalized the verb forms and can move on to producing them in context — for instance, in telling or re-telling stories or in response to questions or topics given to students to talk about for a specified length of time. These are typical activities of TPR Storytelling (see Chapter 4).

Action Series

Single-Tense Series

Series may be done in any tense. It is best for students to have mastered them in a request form before they begin to experience them in any of the tenses. The most commonly used tenses are represented in the following three examples. They can be done in all persons, singular and plural.

Present Continuous

> She's going into the movie theater.
> Now she's looking for a good seat.
> She's watching the movie.
> And now she's clapping.
> (after Romijn and Seely, 1988: 39)

This is always done with the words being spoken as an appropriate person or people are doing the action. The timing is important and often needs attention, especially if some students' native languages, such as Chinese, normally do not express tense. In the above example, the third-person form of the verb is used. The speaker can watch the action while the listener is facing away from it. Notice that *now* and other time and transition expressions may be included.

Simple Past

> First I went into the movie theater.
> Then I looked for a good seat.
> I watched the movie.
> And I clapped.

All the speaking should occur after all the action has been completed. Note again time and transition expressions. Some other useful ones here are *after that, next* and *later.*

"Going to" future and "will" future

> 1. First we're going to go into the movie theater.
>   Next we're going to look for a good seat.
>   After that, we're going to watch the movie.
>   Finally, we're going to clap.
>
> 2. They'll go into the movie theater.
>   And then they'll look for a good seat.
>   And they'll watch the movie.
>   Finally they'll clap.

All the speaking should precede all the action. Note expressions of time and sequence.

Tense Combination Series

The most commonly used tenses — *going to* **future,** *will* **future, present continuous** and **simple past** — are contrasted clearly in this type of exercise which would be used after each of these tenses had been worked on separately. Any two or all three (only one of the futures at a time) may be used in an exercise. Do any one tense first, as done in the above examples. Then do any other. After the second has been practiced, you should practice both together. Finally, add the third, in the next session if you prefer. After practicing it, practice all three together. All deal with the same actions. When all three are combined, the **future** is usually done first, in anticipation of the actions, followed by the **present continuous** as the actions are being performed, and finally the **simple past**, recalling the actions just performed. The **simple present** may be substituted for the present continuous.

To continue using the above three examples, the speaker would say:

> You'll go into the movie theater.
> And then you'll look for a good seat.
> And you'll watch the movie.
> Finally you'll clap.

Listeners do all of these things. As they're doing them, the speaker says:

> You're going into the movie theater.
> You're looking for a good seat.
> You're watching the movie.
> Finally you're clapping.

And after all the action has been completed, the speaker says:

> You went into the movie theater.
> And then you looked for a good seat.
> And you watched the movie.
> Finally you clapped.

All of this can also be said and done action by action:

You'll go into the movie theater.
You're going into the movie theater.
You went into the movie theater.

And then you'll look for a good seat.
You're looking for a good seat.
Then you looked for a good seat.

And you'll watch the movie.
You're watching the movie.
You watched the movie.

Finally you'll clap.
You're clapping.
Finally you clapped.

Jody Klopp's Tense-Acquisition Exercises

Actionlogues (1985) by Joanne "Jody" Klopp consists of 25 action series with a photograph depicting every line (see pp. 23 and 174). She suggests the following exercises for advanced students (in 3rd and 4th years in high school) for the acquisition of tenses:

- To introduce the past tense, set the scene for a day in the past by writing the date on the board. Give a list of commands to a student. The student performs an action, then the teacher describes what happened in the past. "On the 18th day of September, 1963, she yawned." Continue with all the actions in the same manner. Then write the verbs in the past tense on the board. The students will read the verbs from the board this time. Give the acting student another list of the same actions in different order. When the student performs, ask the students, "Did she yawn or did she stretch?" You can use the same type of exercise to introduce the present, future and other tenses. When the students are ready, introduce the tenses with other singular and plural person forms.

- For a written exercise, ask advanced students to write a paragraph that will describe what the person in the photograph did yesterday, will do next week, was doing before you left, would probably do if he had the time, etc....

- Ask a student to go in front of the class and perform 3 or 4 actions of his own choice that he creates. The class divides into 2 groups. After the actor performs, the students decide as a group how to describe the actions the actor performed. The teacher puts a date on the board to determine if their sentence will describe the actions in present, past, or future. The group appoints a spokesperson. The group that comes up with an acceptable interpretation wins points for their team. (p. *iv*)

Berty Segal Cook's Four Levels of Questions

Well-known TPR expert Berty Segal Cook (a.k.a. Berty Segal) has developed a simple, effective way to move from commands to the basic tenses — the present or present continuous, the past used to express that someone did something one time, and the future. This solution to the transition from the imperative to tenses is based on the Natural Approach (Terrell and Krashen, 1983). Using vocabulary that students are very familiar with and that they have experienced with action, the teacher tells one or more students to do a few actions. Depending on the tense, s/he describes the actions that are acted out by the student(s) (1) while they are acting them out (present continuous or present), (2) after they have finished acting them out (past) or (3) before they act them out (future). Then s/he has them perform the actions again and asks questions of students at the appropriate time.

There are four levels of questions. The 1st-level question elicits only a one-word answer by the students — just *yes* or *no* or a name. In the 1st and 2nd levels, the answer is essentially contained in the question. At the 3rd level, only part of it is in the question; the students must come up with the other part of the answer. At the 4th level the students must come up with everything and produce a complete sentence. Below is the summary of the four levels given in her book *Teaching English Through Action*

(1992: 9), which is available in several languages (see Segal in the bibliography):

Level 1: Who is sitting?
         Is Juan sitting?
         Who is tapping his head ?
(Teacher provides vocabulary; students respond with *yes/no* or name (Juan).)

Level 2: Is (s)he sitting or standing?
         Is she tapping her head or her nose?
(Teacher provides vocabulary; students respond with verb or a noun.)

Level 3: Where is (s)he sitting?
         What is (s)he tapping?
(Teacher provides partial vocabulary; students respond with 3-word phrase "on the chair.")

Level 4: What is (s)he doing?
(Student provides vocabulary.)

"Horizontal" Learning of Verb Forms

This is the term used by the late Paul Pimsleur in *How to Learn a Foreign Language* (Boston: Heinle & Heinle, 1980: 55-57) to refer to the learning, for example, of the forms of the first-person singular for many verbs all together — including forms from all conjugations as well as irregular forms (as opposed to the traditional way of "learning" all persons together — the vertical list of six forms, 1st-, 2nd- & 3rd-persons, singular & plural — of a single irregular verb or of a particular conjugation). For example, in Spanish the first-person singular forms *miro* (I'm looking, I look), *como* (I'm eating, I eat) and *abro* (I'm opening, I open) — all of which are from different conjugations — can be practiced along with *tengo* (I have), which is an irregular verb.

Pimsleur was not suggesting the use of TPR. Nonetheless, horizontal learning of verb forms can be accomplished with TPR, as in the following example of the present tense: Students observe the teacher doing various actions while using the first-person singular form to describe his/her own actions. The teacher does this in a few different class sessions while the students observe. Then the students do the same, acting and speaking along with the teacher. And then a few volunteers or quicker students do it alone. Finally everyone does it in pairs, one person in each pair acting and speaking at a time, while the other observes. The same treatment is subsequently given to forms for each of the various persons, singular and plural, as appropriate individuals or pairs act and speak. Question structures are also practiced, along with appropriate answer forms. For example, two persons may perform the action of eating while another asks them, "Are you eating?" and they answer, "Yes, we're eating." Or, alternatively the question might be "Are you walking?" and the answer "No, we're eating."

Compare this procedure with those described above in this chapter on pp. 113-114 in the section entitled "TPR Storytelling" and on pp. 115-118 in the section called "Action Series."

A Note on the Nesting of Tenses in the Imperative

Asher (see 1996: pp. 3-42 and 3-43) and others advocate the nesting of grammatical structures in sentences in which the imperative is the main verb. The purpose of nesting is to allow students to understand and internalize forms of verbs other than the imperative. For example, the sentence *Pick up the umbrella that June threw on the floor* contains the past form *threw*. And *Wave to the girl who will travel to New Zealand* contains the future. Experience shows that for most students nesting alone is not an effective means of achieving acquisition of such forms to the point where they can be reliably produced in conversation. Something else must be done, or most students — although they will comprehend the non-imperative form — will not internalize it or subsequently produce it. Pointing out the new forms and writing them on the board or the overhead helps. Even more important is to use them in some "natural" context so that students have the opportunity both to comprehend the circumstances in which they are used and to use them in such circumstances. All of the ways of acquiring tenses that are mentioned in this chapter provide contexts that are to one degree or another natural. They are effective whether nesting is used or not — as long as students have by some means previously internalized the vocabulary they are using. As is the case with all material, familiarity with such forms makes it easier for students to acquire them.

A frequent problem is that the verb form is only minimally different from the imperative and that many students may not notice the difference when they hear it pronounced. Many ESL students have this problem with the past form *-ed*, for example. On the other hand, sometimes a non-imperative form is irregular and so different from the imperative that students don't even recognize it as a form of the same verb, e.g., *bought* in English and *fue* in Spanish. It is essential to point out both of these types of cases.

Other Ways of Dealing with the
Acquisition of Tenses and Verb Forms

For other ways of dealing with the acquisition of tenses and verb forms through TPR, you may wish to consult some of the numerous works listed in the references and bibliography on pp. 168-177, in particular Eric Schessler's *English Grammar Through Actions* (1984; also available in Spanish and French), the lessons developed by Carol Adamski in Part IV of Asher's *Learning Another Language Through Actions* (1996), *Instructor's Notebook* by Ramiro García (1988), Stephen Silvers' *Listen and Perform* (1985), and *Total Physical Response in First Year Spanish* by Francisco Cabello (1985; also available in English and French).

Chapter 6:
Acquiring Other Grammatical Features and Idioms and Expressions with TPR

Most of this chapter consists of natural action dialogs. We suggest you consult "Natural Action Dialogs" on pages 28-32 for further information about using such material. Note that it is often useful to employ a TPR dictation (see pp. 139-141) in connection with student oral/aural practice of natural action dialogs and that in some circumstances doing some work on pronunciation is worthwhile.

INDEFINITE AND NEGATIVE PRONOUNS

Some action series lend themselves to practicing **indefinite** and **negative pronouns**. This can actually be done in any verb tense, but here is how it can go in the simple past, using "Painting a Picture" (Romijn and Seely, 1988: 18):

Have a different person perform each step of the series (see the natural action dialog for the simple past on pp. 95-96 in Chapter 5, "Acquiring Tenses" for more about how to do this). Then ask *wh-* questions about the students who *did* the actions. After each of these questions, ask the same question about another student who *didn't* do the action. At first provide the answers yourself. Then keep doing it and have students respond *en masse*:

1. Where did Juan spread out the newspapers?
   He spread them out on the desk.

2. Where did Xiao spread out the newspapers?
   Nowhere.
   also: She didn't spread them out *anywhere*.

3. What did Sonja take out?
   She took out a piece of paper.

4. What did Gustaf take out?
   Nothing.
   also: He didn't take out *anything*.

5. Which jar of paint did you open?
   I opened the blue jar.

6. Which jar did he open?
   None of them.
   also: He didn't open *any* of them.
   or (if there are only two jars of paint):
   Neither one.
   He didn't open *either* jar.

You may find it useful to do a dictation before having students practice in pairs (see "TPR Dictation," pp. 139-141). It is a good idea to do this same exercise with many different action series over a period of many class sessions.

COUNT AND NON-COUNT NOUNS AND
COMPARATIVES AND SUPERLATIVES

(PLEASE NOTE: These particular distinctions may not be relevant
if you are not teaching English.)

Bring to class:

    a. A large container of water.

    b. very small clear containers (plastic cups)
one for each student.

    c. A bag of beans (or any other cheap, safe, small ob-
ject; very small nails (2-3 pounds are good for
adults; don't use nails with kids or young playful
adults))

COMPARATIVES & SUPERLATIVES
WITH NON-COUNT NOUNS

Set up:

Pour each student some water, telling them not to
drink it and trying to put a different amount in each
cup — some only a few drops, some a small trickle,
some full to the top and every amount in between.

Ask each student:

Do you have *a little* water or *a lot* of water?

or: Do you have *a little* or *a lot*?

Write these two questions on the board or overhead, underlining *a little* and *a lot* and *a little water* and *a lot of water*. Be
sure they all understand the meanings.

Pair practice:

Have them ask each other the questions.

Practice this also in the **3rd person**:

Does Anna have a little or a lot?

125

Compare:

Now ask them to compare:

> Who has *more* water, you or Li?

> *and*: Who has *less* water, you or Li?

Write these questions on the board, underlining the words *more* and *less*.

Now write *more than* and *less than* on the board. Ask the same questions again, prompting students to give full answers.

Pair practice:

Have them ask each other the questions.

Where two people seem to have equal amounts of water, point this out to everybody and teach them the expression *We have* **the same amount**.

Write this sentence on the board also and have everyone practice it in pairs, referring to two people who actually do have the same amount: "Billo and Lynda have the same amount."

Natural action dialog:

Take a cup with only a little water for yourself and go to a student with a lot. Ask:

> T: Can I have *some more* water?

> S: (pours some into your cup:)

> T: Oh, that's *too much*! Here, take a little *back*.

> S: (pours some back into his/her cup)

Write the spoken lines on the board.

Have several pairs practice them while everyone else watches.

Pair practice:

Then have everyone practice them in pairs. Be sure that they all understand that *they must do the action, that without the action it's all meaningless*.

Here is another action dialog to do in the same fashion:

T: Can I have *some more* water?

S: (pours some into your cup)

T: Oh, that's *not enough*! Give me *a little more*!

S: (pours you more)

Again, it is important to keep reminding students that they should do the *actions* in natural action dialogs, that the words refer to their actions and, if the actions are not done, the words are meaningless.

Superlatives:

Before you collect the water, ask the whole group:

Who has *the most* water?

Who has *the least* water?

Show everybody as you exclaim:

Dhakel has the most.

Rosario has the least.

Pair practice:

Tell the whole class to stand up, and have everyone move around the room, asking these questions of 3 or 4 other students.

Paradigm:

Write this paradigm on the board:

a little	less than	the least
a lot	more than	the most

and discuss and show the differences in meaning and use.

What you have done above is teach and provide hands-on practice with *a non-count noun*. What follows is a similar treatment of *a count noun*: You may do it immediately in the same class session, or you may do it in the following one. If you do it the same one, collect the water *before* you pass out the beans or nails (or you'll have soggy beans or rusty nails in no time!).

COMPARATIVES & SUPERLATIVES
WITH COUNT NOUNS

Pass out the beans:

Give each student a different number of beans, from just one
or two to a large handful or two. Tell the students to count
how many beans they have.

Ask each student:

How many beans do you have?

Do you have *a lot* of beans or *a few*?

How many beans does Xiao have?

Does Xiao have *a lot* or *a few*?

Comparing count nouns:

Explain that for something you can count, like beans, you talk
about *a lot* or *a few*, but with something you can't count, like
water, you talk about *a lot* or *a little*.

Now ask individuals:

Who has *more* beans, you or me?

Who has *fewer* beans, you or Sonja?

(You may wish to point out that the word *less* is often
used in speech in place of the word *fewer*.)

Where you notice some students have *the same number* of
beans, write this phrase on the board and compare to *the
same amount*.

Natural action dialogs:

Repeat the natural action dialogs from above, changing *water* to *beans*.

Can I have *some more* beans?

Oh, that's too *many*! Here, take *a few* back.

and:

Can I have some more beans?

Oh, that's not enough! Give me *a few* more.

Superlative form for count nouns:

Before collecting the beans, ask the whole group:

Who has *the most* beans?

Who has *the fewest* beans?

(Here again, you may want to mention *least*.)

Ask the above questions of 3 or 4 other people.

Pair practice:

Tell the whole class to stand up, and have everyone move around the room, asking these questions of 3 or 4 other students.

Paradigm:

Write this paradigm on the board:

a few	fewer than	the fewest
a lot	more than	the most

Again, go over the differences in meaning. Then compare this paradigm to the previous one for non-count nouns.

MORE PRACTICE

DISTINGUISHING COUNT AND NON-COUNT NOUNS:

Name various familiar nouns and/or show some things and/or illustrations, mixing count and non-count:

sugar	perfume
children	money
minutes	dollars
time	love
apples	kisses
fruit	students

and ask the students whether each should be:

a few	or	*a little?*
not many	or	*not much?*
how many	or	*how much?*
the same number of	or	*the same amount of?*

Point out that *a lot, more than* and *the most* are all used with both count and non-count nouns.

Group Work:

Divide the class into groups of 3-5 people. Have each group put together a list of 10 nouns that they use in their own lives. Tell them to include count and non-count nouns. Each student should make his/her own copy of the list.

Pair Practice:

When they are ready, have the students leave their groups and find a partner from a different group. Students are now in pairs rather than groups. Put the following statements and questions on the board before they begin this pair practice and give a few examples of how to select an appropriate one for each noun presented:

I don't have many _____ .
I don't have much _____ .

I have a few _____ .
I have a lot of _____ .

How many _____ do you have?
How much _____ do you have?

We have the same number of _____ .
We have the same amount of _____ .

You have more _____ than me.
I have more _____ than you.

Have the students present their lists to each other orally by using each noun in one of the above sentences.

Close any of the above steps with a dictation of any of the sentences used. (See "TPR Dictation," pp. 139-141.)

PAST PARTICIPLES AS ADJECTIVES

Hand a piece of paper to one student and ask her to tear it:

Juanita, please tear this paper.

Hand a different piece of paper to another student to fold:

Julio, please fold this paper.

Collect the two pieces of paper and ask the class (holding up the torn paper, then the folded one):

Who tore this paper? (Juanita did.)

Who folded this paper? (Julio did.)

Write the paradigms:

tear	tore	torn
fold	folded	folded

on the board and be sure the students understand their meanings, giving more examples, especially for the past participles:

I *haven't torn* any paper today.

My brother *has already folded* the clean clothes.

Now hand the torn paper and the folded paper to two different students. Hand a piece of yellow (or any color) paper to another and a small (or large or long) piece of paper to another. Ask:

Who has the yellow paper?

Who has the small paper?

Who has the folded paper?

Who has the torn paper?

Point out that the words *yellow*, *small*, *folded* and *torn* are all *adjectives*, words that describe nouns. In this case they are describing paper and distinguishing four different pieces. Also point out that *folded* and *torn* are the past participles of the verbs and that we often use this form as an adjective (this is also done in many other languages, so a translation of a few words would be useful here, if appropriate). Give a few other examples of verbs the students already know, and ask students if they can think of more.

> a burned match
>
> a closed door
>
> a cooked hamburger
>
> a wrapped present
>
> a half-eaten pizza
>
> a cut flower
>
> a peeled banana
>
> a surprised teacher
>
> a hidden purse
>
> a stolen wallet
>
> a written exercise
>
> a tied balloon
>
> a beaten egg
>
> a scared child

Practice

Now ask everyone to take out two pieces of paper. Have them all *tear* one piece and *fold* the other. Now tell them to:

> Put the torn paper on top of the folded paper.
>
> Put the folded paper on your head.
>
> Put the torn paper in the folded paper.
>
> Put the folded paper under your chair.

And ask them:

> Where is the folded paper?
>
> Where is the torn paper?

Have individuals give similar instructions and the same questions to you while the others listen. Then have them give the instructions and ask the questions to each other, working in pairs. Close with a dictation of any of the sentences used. (See "TPR Dictation," pp. 139-141.)

For an effective way of teaching possessive adjectives, see p. 92.

ADVERBS

(intermediate level)

Ask the students to do one of the actions in a series *slowly*. Ask them to do the same action *fast*. Ask them to do it *calmly*, then *nervously*. If they hesitate, demonstrate these ways yourself, exaggerating the differences. (Here's where the ham in you really gets to shine!)

Compare the **adjectives**:

> *slow, fast, calm, nervous*

with the **adverbs**:

> *slowly, fast, calmly, nervously*

Explain the differences in meaning between the **adjectives** and the **adverbs** and give examples of how the adjectives are used to describe *nouns* or *things* (a slow *horse*, a fast *car*, a calm *baby*, a nervous *patient*), and the adverbs are used to describe *verbs* or *actions*, that is, they tell *how*, the *manner* or *way* that an action is performed. Demonstrate the actions in these four manners again. Write *slowly*, walk *fast*, close the window *calmly*, close the door *nervously*. Then point out that in English most (but not all) adverbs are similar to adjectives in form but with *-ly* added to the end. (If you are teaching Spanish rather than English, point out that the feminine singular form of the adjective is what *-mente* is attached to and give examples.) Translate a few of these pairs (*slow — slowly*; *calm — calmly*) into the students' native language(s) if possible and if it seems that this will help clarify the difference.

Now introduce some more **adjective/adverb pairs** to demonstrate the **spelling rule** of changing *-y* to *-i* (*happy — happily*; *angry — angrily*) and demonstrate doing some actions happily and sadly, angrily and nicely. Add more adverbs to the list.

Here are some suggestions:

neatly	sloppily
gracefully	clumsily

gradually	suddenly
timidly	confidently, proudly
quietly	noisily
softly	loudly
lazily	energetically
carefully	carelessly

List them on the board and discuss and demonstrate the meaning and show the adjective from which the adverb is derived if it is not familiar or obvious. (Be sure they don't confuse *confidently* with *confidentially* — stress that this is the opposite of *timidly;* demonstrate one action done *timidly* and then *confidently*.)

Next, go through a series asking various students each to pantomime a different step, and each in a different manner. For example (from "Cheese" in Romijn and Seely, 1988: 4):

Sonja, unwrap the cheese *clumsily.*

Jesús, put it on the cutting board *angrily.*

Gustaf, pick up the knife *happily.*

Anna, cut a little piece of cheese *timidly.*

Encourage them to exaggerate the manner dramatically. To do this, have the students *guess* what adverb you or another student is demonstrating without stating it first. The manner will probably have to be very exaggerated to get the meaning across.

Then state the declarative sentences about all actions and manners which were demonstrated, so that students will hear how the adverbs are used in sentences:

Sonja unwrapped the cheese clumsily.

Jesús put it on the cutting board angrily.

Gustaf picked up the knife happily.

Anna cut a little piece of cheese timidly.

"IN THE MANNER OF THE ADVERB" — THE GAME

You are now ready to play a game called *"In the Manner of the Adverb."* Send one student ("IT") out of the room, while everyone else decides on one adverb for this round of the game. When this has been accomplished, have IT return to the room to discover which adverb you have agreed upon.

Now IT must ask someone to do a specific action from the lesson "in the manner of the adverb." For example, IT might ask a student to *unwrap the cheese* in the manner of the adverb (or in a certain way). If the adverb selected is *noisily*, that student should proceed to make as much noise as possible while unwrapping the cheese.

IT can now guess which adverb is being demonstrated, or ask a different student to do a different specified action in the manner of the adverb. IT can in this way ask for as many demonstrations as it takes to understand and guess what adverb has been selected by the group. When IT identifies the adverb correctly, have another IT go out of the room and select a different adverb.

After each IT guesses his/her adverb correctly, summarize with declarative sentences the actions done by the various students all in the same manner. For example:

Paolo unwrapped the cheese noisily.

Silvia took a bite noisily.

Thi chewed it up noisily.

Ask the students if they can remember and state the rest of the actions done in that round of the game.

If you have a little time before the end of class, you might want to dictate one sentence from each round while the students write them, in order to practice spelling.

"QUICKIE" NATURAL ACTION DIALOGS

Three or more simple commands are practiced:

- Go out to dinner. (With an illustration of a restaurant.)
- Wipe off your desk.
- Buy something. (With an illustration of a store.)

The illustrations serve as cues to aid in recalling options. Then the following "quickie" natural action dialog is practiced by the teacher and a student or two, and the chosen action is performed after it is mentioned:

135

1: What would you like to do?

2: I'd like to _____ .

Then students practice in pairs.

Idioms and expressions can be practiced in the same manner. To practice the expression *Good idea!*, place some illustrations of places around the room. Then practice the following quickie natural action dialog with a student or two:

1: Let's go to the _____ , okay?

2: Good idea! Let's go!

To practice *Is that all?* and *That's all*, provide a few objects to be counted. Then practice this quickie with one or two students before pair practice:

1: Count your _____s.

2: 1, 2, ...

1: How many _____s have you got?

2: 5.

1: Is that all?

2: Yeah, that's all.

USING SINGLE COMMANDS AND DESCRIPTIONS TO ACQUIRE EXPRESSIONS

Idioms and other expressions can be acquired through strategic use of single commands and descriptions in monologues. To practice *a long way* and *not very far away*, place on the wall toward the back of the classroom, a map or rough drawing of a far-off place, say Africa if you are in Tokyo. Place at the front of the room a map or drawing to represent a nearby city or town, say Yokohama. Then give the following commands and descriptions to the whole class:

Go to Yokohama.

Come back fast — in half an hour.

Yokohama's *not very far away*.

Go to Africa.

Come back fast — in *two* days.

Africa's *a long way*.

More places can be added. The distances can be exaggerated through the movements and gestures of the physical respondents. After students have internalized the expressions, have one or two deliver a similar monologue to you. Then have students practice in pairs.

ACQUIRING GRAMMATICAL FEATURES THROUGH TPR STORYTELLING

Short phrases containing grammatical features can be presented, according to Blaine Ray, "as vocabulary," meaning that they can be presented and internalized through hand TPR (see pp. 44-49. For example, a possessive adjective can be introduced in a phrase as a vocabulary item, e.g., *my flower*, with a hand sign used to represent the phrase. Or, the normal position of adjectives in French can be presented with a simple phrase like *le livre bleu* (the blue book). Idiomatic phrases like the Spanish *hace sol* (it is sunny) can also be introduced and internalized in the same way.

In the process of students learning to tell a story, "guide words" are utilized to make sure students pay attention to and produce such features (see pp. 58-62). The acquisition of a grammatical feature occurs over time, as more similar items are dealt with in the same way. As a feature is used over and over again in different contexts, it is gradually acquired, often without students even being aware that they are acquiring a grammatical element. It just comes to sound right to them, as in first language acquisition. Continued comprehensible input is another key factor in this process. The use of guide words to achieve acquisition applies not only to short, simple features, but also to complex sentence-long structures such as *If I were a carpenter, I would make you a see-saw*.

Other Ways of Dealing with the
Acquisition of Grammatical Features

For other ways of dealing with the acquisition of grammatical features through TPR, you may wish to consult some of the numerous works listed in the references and bibliography on pp. 168-177, in particular Eric Schessler's *English Grammar Through Actions* (1984; also available in Spanish and French).

Chapter 7:

Writing, Pronunciation, Reading and Assessment

THE TPR DICTATION

What can you accomplish with the TPR Dictation?

1. It *clarifies* and *reinforces* aural work, provides additional aural input. Allows students to *focus on details* of both grammar and writing.

2. It *introduces* spelling, punctuation, function words.

3. It can be used as a basis for *explanations* of

   a. Grammar rules.

   b. Spelling rules.

   c. Pronunciation problems.

4. It can be used as a basis for *practice* of

   a. Grammar points

   b. Pronunciation.

5. All this can be done *within context*, without divorcing any aspect of language from meaning or comprehension.

6. It will be done at different points within the lesson, depending upon the age, level and aptitudes of the students.

a. *Children* will do physical, aural, oral practice much longer before getting dictation than will adults.

b. For *adults*, learners who are more communicative aurally/orally will learn more from dictation and will benefit from doing it earlier on in the lesson than will students who already communicate better on paper.

c. In more *advanced lessons*, when more complicated structures are used, dictation can be used early on as additional aural input *before* the students attempt utterances themselves. The dictation can then be practiced orally if the students seem ready, or not if they don't. If they do practice it, they'll be practicing something meaningful, in context, but before they actually have to *create* their own utterances with the new patterns.

7. It gives closure to the lesson and gives the students a sense of satisfaction and confidence.

8. It is a terrific *assessment* tool, not only of the students' progress but of your lesson as well. As you dictate sentences, go around the room to see how well the students are writing. You may learn a lot about what they do or do not understand!

PROCEDURES FOR THE TPR DICTATION

1. **Present an oral TPR lesson** of any type (use all procedures for that type.)

2. Be sure the students have been provided with all **written** words they'll need for dictation (on board, in text and/or from previous lessons.)

3. **Give the dictation**

   a. Use only sentences already practiced in the TPR lesson.

   b. Refer to context, if possible, during dictation. Often you can actually *have the sentence enacted* just before you say it as dictation. This is extremely effective. For instance, using "Vitamin Pill" (see p. 22) as the series on which the dictation is based and the simple past tense as the structure point being dealt with, you tell a student: "Emiliano, swallow the pill." After he has done the action in pantomime so that everyone could see him doing it, you say, "He swallowed the pill. Write this. Number one: He swallowed the pill." This can be done just as easily for the simple present, the present continuous (present progressive), the future with *going to* or *will*, the present perfect.

   c. If dictating questions, you may either dictate the answers you want them to practice writing, or have students write their own answers.

   d. Use pronunciation and speed as close to normal as they can handle, as well as slower speeds, for clarity.

   e. Go around and look at their papers to see how they're doing.

   f. Repeat as many times as needed — this is not a test, but a learning exercise.

4. **Correct** together

   a. Volunteers write individual lines on the board.

   b. Teacher corrects errors with the whole group.

   c. Students correct their own papers or each others'.

5. **Point out** spelling and punctuation rules, grammar points and pronunciation problems (and practice these.)

6. Pair practice (if appropriate) of what they've just written.

WRITTEN EXERCISES AND QUIZZES

Following are excerpts from a variety of written exercises or quizzes that are for the most part based on material that has been previously internalized by students through physical response to commands. PLEASE NOTE: The great majority of the content comes from action series in *Live Action English* (1988: Romijn and Seely). Titles of action series and page numbers are given with the exercises. For the Spanish, French, Japanese, German and Italian versions, in most cases the equivalent action series can be found by doubling the page number given for the English version.

VOCABULARY ("Sharpening Your Pencil," p. 9)

Select the best conclusion for each sentence. CIRCLE IT.

EXAMPLE: *Little* is the opposite of
a) dirty.   b) new.   c) big.

1. Your *thumb* is one of your
a) ears.   b) fingers.   c) legs.

2. You *sharpen* your pencil when it's
a) clean.   b) wet.   c) dull.

3. When you *borrow* something, you
a) give it back later.   b) keep it.   c) steal it.

VERB TENSES ("Good Morning," p. 14)

Connect each sentence with the correct time:

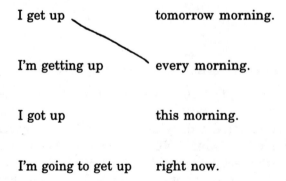

I get up   tomorrow morning.

I'm getting up   every morning.

I got up   this morning.

I'm going to get up   right now.

VERB FORMS ("Good Morning," p. 14)

How do you spell the *-ing form* and the *past form* for each verb?

	-ing	past
EXAMPLE: get	*getting*	*got*
1. wake	_____	_____
2. rub	_____	_____
3. do	_____	_____
4. go	_____	_____
5. brush	_____	_____
6. kiss	_____	_____

WRITING ("Good Morning," p. 14)

Please write *complete* answers to the questions:

Every day

1. What time do you get up?

   _____

2. Do you make the bed *before* or *after* you eat breakfast?

   _____

3. What do you eat in the morning?

   _____

4. Do you read the newspaper?

   _____

POSSESSIVES ("Washing Your Hands," p. 1,
or "Good Morning," p. 14)

Complete each sentence with the correct possessive form:

EXAMPLE: I'm washing _my_ hands.

1. She's washing _____ hands.

2. You're washing _____ hands.

3. He's washing _____ hands.

4. We're washing _____ hands.

5. They're washing _____ hands.

VOCABULARY

What do you call this?

(10 previously internalized objects are displayed, each with a number attached to it.)

PAST FORMS ("Scrambled Eggs," p. 34)

Complete two answers for each question:

1. What did you *fix* for breakfast yesterday?

I _____ scrambled eggs.

You didn't _____ anything.

2. How many eggs did you *break*?

I _____ three eggs.

You didn't _____ any eggs.

3. Where did you *drop* them?

I _____ them into a bowl.

She didn't _____ them.

4. What did you *pick* up?

I _____ up the egg beater.

They didn't _____ up anything.

5. What did you *beat*?

I _____ the eggs.

She didn't _____ anything.

SHORT ANSWERS ("A Jack-O-Lantern for Halloween,"
p. 66; "Taking Care of a Baby," p. 25;
"Going to the Movies," p. 39)

Complete each answer.

EXAMPLE:
Are we playing Bingo?   No, we *aren't* .

1. Is today Halloween?   No, it _____ .

2. Is the baby messy?   Yes, she _____ .

3. Did you kiss the baby?   Yes, I _____ .

4. Was the movie scary?   Yes, it _____ .

5. Do you like scary movies? No, I _____ .

6. Does your mother go to the movies every week?

No, she _____ .

PRONOUNS ("Washing Your Hands," p. 1;
          "Taking Care of a Baby," p. 25)

Select the correct word and circle it.

EXAMPLE: I'm looking for   (her.)

she.

1. Do you have   me / my   book?

me

1. Do you have   book?

   my

   me

2. Please give   the book.

   my

  your

3. Where is   mother?

  you're

He's

4.   baby is crying.

His

      him.

5. Please give the baby to

      his.

  us

6. We're washing   hands.

  our

7.
  They're   washing   they're   hands.
  Their   their

8. I have something for   you.

                                      your.

WRITING ("Car Ride," p. 54)

Write 3 sentences about your car:

[Students who do not have cars can make something up.]

_____

_____

_____

WHICH QUESTION IS CORRECT?
  ("Grocery Shopping," p. 41)

Circle the correct question.

1. I have an apple.

    a. How much does it weigh?

    b. How much do they weigh?

2. I'm buying some eggs.

    a. How much does it cost?

    b. How much do they cost?

3. I have some bananas.

    a. How much does it weigh?

    b. How much do they weigh?

CATEGORIES ("Grocery Shopping," p. 41)

Look at this list: potato, banana, peach, grapes, carrots, corn, beets, pineapple, melon, cauliflower

1. Which ones are fruits?_____

_____

_____

2. Which ones are vegetables?_____

_____

_____

SAME OR DIFFERENT? ("Car Ride," p. 54)

Write D if the two words have a DIFFERENT meaning.
Write S if the two words have a SIMILAR meaning:

EXAMPLE:
    name   address   *D*

1. release   let go   _____

2. change   shift   _____

3. roll down   pull over   _____

4. engine   motor   _____

5. start   begin   _____

WRITING ("Eating Oranges," p. 44)

How do you usually eat an orange?

_____

_____

_____

_____

PRESENT CONTINUOUS ("Using a Pay Phone," p. 30)
(see "Practice of negative forms" in the present continuous natural action dialogs on pp. 93-95 of Chapter 5, "Acquiring Tenses" in this book)

Complete the dialogs:

— Go into the phone booth.

Don't _____ into the bathroom!

— I'm _____ _____ into bathroom.

— Where _____ you _____ ?

— _____ _____ into the phone booth.

— Wait a few minutes.

Don't _____ an hour!

— I'm _____ _____ an hour.

— How long _____ you _____ ?

— _____ _____ a few minutes.

PRESENT CONTINUOUS ("Going to the Movies," p. 39)

For each picture, answer two questions.

EXAMPLE:

What's he doing? *He's screaming.*

Why? *Because the movie is scary.*

1. What's he doing? _____

   Why? _____

2. What's he doing? _____

   Why? _____

3. What's he doing? _____

   Why? _____

4. What's he doing? _____

   Why? _____

COUNT/NON-COUNT (see pp. 125-130 in this book)

How much or *How many?*   *a little* or *a few?*

1. How _____ money do you have?

   I only have a _____ .

2. How _____ dollars do you have?

   I only have a _____ .

3. How _____ teachers do you have?

I only have a _____ .

4. How _____ education do you have?

I only have a _____ .

COMPARATIVES AND SUPERLATIVES
(see pp. 125-130 in this book)

Select the correct word to complete each sentence.

EXAMPLE: This class has （more） students than the other class.
most

                less
1. She has   money than you.
                least

                less
2. I have the   money of all.
                least

                more
3. They have   children than we do.
                most

                more
4. She has the   children of anybody in this class.
                most

fewer

5. We eat   oranges than you.

fewest

fewer

6. He eats the   oranges of all the people at his job.

fewest

COMPARISONS (see pp. 125-130 in this book)

Look at the picture and answer the questions.

DOUG'S WATER   SUSAN'S WATER   MARK'S WATER

1. Who has more water, Doug or Susan?

_____

2. Who has less water, Doug or Susan?

_____

3. Who has the most water?

_____

4. Who has the least water?

_____

MARGE'S APPLES   DAVE'S APPLES   CAROLYN'S APPLES

5. Who has more apples, Marge or Dave?

_____

6. Who has fewer apples, Dave or Carolyn?

_____

7. Who has the most apples?

_____

8. Who has the fewest apples?

_____

PRONUNCIATION AND LISTENING DISCRIMINATION

Following are a few pronunciation and listening discrimination exercises in English, all of which are based on material previously internalized through TPR commands, particularly through the use of action series. We have found that it is generally far more effective to deal with pronunciation continually in context rather than drilling it out of context. Refer to pp. 96-97 for an effective way of getting students to acquire the three different pronunciations of -ed in English in context.

PRONUNCIATION

What letters are not pronounced? CIRCLE THEM.

EXAMPLE: nic(e)   thum(b)   hol(e)

          clean   write   coat

          inside   buy   bought

          looked   tried

LISTENING

Listen to the teacher. Circle the word that you hear.

EXAMPLE:

    a. like   b. lick   (c. liked)   d. licked

1. a. wait   b. weigh   c. waited   d. weighed

2. a. wait   b. weigh   c. waited   d. weighed

3. a. wait   b. weigh   c. waited   d. weighed

4. a. wait   b. weigh   c. waited   d. weighed

5. a. back   b. bag   c. bagged

6. a. back   b. bag   c. bagged

7. a. back   b. bag   c. bagged

8. a. star b. start c. started

9. a. star b. start c. started

10. a. star b. start c. started

11. a. wash b. washed c. watch d. watched

12. a. wash b. washed c. watch d. watched

13. a. wash b. washed c. watch d. watched

14. a. wash b. washed c. watch d. watched

PRONUNCIATION — PAST FORMS

What is the past form for each verb?
Is the past form pronounced with one syllable or two?

	basic form	past form	1 syllable	2 syllables
EXAMPLE:	put	*put*	X	___
1.	need	___	___	___
2.	cash	___	___	___
3.	walk	___	___	___
4.	go	___	___	___
5.	write	___	___	___
6.	sign	___	___	___
7.	get	___	___	___
8.	wait	___	___	___
9.	move	___	___	___
10.	hand	___	___	___
11.	say	___	___	___
12.	take	___	___	___
13.	count	___	___	___

PRONUNCIATION

Listen to the teacher. Is her/his pronunciation *right* or *wrong*?

	right	wrong
EXAMPLE A: cut	X	
EXAMPLE B: cut [coot]		X
1. first [feerst]		
2. first		
3. half [half]		
4. half [hæf]		
5. bite [beet]		
6. bite		
7. pulp		
8. pulp [poolp]		

READING

Stories and factual types of reading materials based on content previously internalized through TPR can be useful for obvious reasons such as reinforcement, expansion of passive vocabulary and reading practice. You may wish to create your own. You may also wish to enlist the aid of students in creating such materials.

There are books which have high-interest stories based on TPR lessons:

- All of the student books at different levels by Blaine Ray et al. in the *Look, I Can Talk!* series (1990, 1992, 1993) in English, Spanish, French and German. Also, the brief first-year Spanish novel by Ray's sister Lisa Ray Turner and himself, *Casi se muere* (1998).

- *¡Cuéntame!* (1994) and *¡Cuéntame más!* (1994) in Spanish and *Raconte-moi!* (1994), *Raconte-moi encore!*

(1995) in French and *Tell Me More* (1998) in English (ESL adaptation by Carol Gaab) by Valeri Marsh (a.k.a. Valeri Waxman-Marsh) and Christine Anderson.

- *TPR Student Kit Stories* (1994) in English by Joan Rosen.

See the bibliography for more details on these books.

ASSESSMENT/TESTING

The most important thing to keep in mind regarding assessment, or testing, is that the teacher can learn from it (1) what has worked in the activities of a class and in the ways the class has been run and (2) what needs to be done differently and what needs more work.

There are various ways of assessing or testing what students are able to accomplish in the "four skills." The simplest and most obvious is merely to give them commands — spoken or in writing — and see if they can respond to them physically. This is for the receptive skills. For productive skills, a similarly simple procedure is to do the opposite. The teacher performs an action, and the student — through either speech or writing — describes it or produces the command (which then can be performed again by the teacher). Illustrations can also be used to elicit speech or writing.

One point worth noting about testing/assessment of listening comprehension is that for the most part it is not necessary with TPR. The teacher can see whether students are responding correctly and quickly or not. Of course, there is the possibility that students will just imitate the crowd, not paying attention to the words. If individual students are asked to carry out commands at times — especially some of the less sharp students — this problem is avoided. There is also a danger that a student will overgeneralize or undergeneralize an action, for example that s/he will think that *walk* means *go* and vice versa. This too can be. avoided by various simple means, such as by being careful about the precise movements used when presenting or clarifying the meaning of an item, by repeating the presentation of an item in various contexts or by quick translation. See "Ways and Means of Getting Across Meaning" (pp. 26-28).

We will not go into assessment/testing in depth here, but we suggest you consult *Instructor's Notebook: How to Apply TPR for Best Results* (1988) and *The Graphics Book* (1991) by Ramiro García, *Teaching English Through Action* by Berty Segal (1992), Asher's own *Learning Another Language Through Actions* (1996), and Kay Price and Marge Dequine's Quick Start in English program (see p. 177 for the last one). Also see *Fluency through TPR Storytelling* by Blaine Ray and Contee Seely (1998). Please see the references and the bibliography.

Chapter 8:
Overcoming Problems

Adaptation

Resistance may occur after a while when some students get tired of moving in response to commands, or just get tired of moving, or just get tired of doing the same thing. They cease to find it fun and interesting. Asher applies the term *adaptation*, from biology, to this phenomenon. He gives the following definition of it in *Learning Another Language Through Actions*: "Adaptation is the phenomenon in which one discontinues making a response to a continual stimulus" (Asher, 1996: page 3-53).

In his discussion of adaptation on pages 3-53 to 3-56, he mentions what he thinks are the two best ways to deal with it. One is to set short-term "operational" student goals, i.e., goals that state that students will be able to accomplish certain specified tasks by a specified time. The second of the two best ways to deal with adaptation, according to Asher, is to continually switch back and forth between right-brain and left-brain activities. He calls this "brainswitching."

An example of a short-term operational goal and how to use brainswitching in accomplishing it is:

In two weeks students will be able to do the following in Spanish in relation to a visit to a Mexican restaurant: "(a) call up and make a reservation, (b) explain who we are

when we get there, (c) order our meals, (d) ask about the
location of the restrooms, and (e) pay our checks."

Asher, 1996: page 3-55

Other examples of such goals "that are *attractive to students*"
[Asher's emphasis] are "reading the headlines in a Japanese
newspaper, ordering breakfast from a German menu, understanding three TV commercials from Spain, buying a bus ticket
in China, giving directions to a taxi driver in France." (Asher,
1996: page 3-32) Asher suggests that teachers ask students to
suggest such goals. Each goal chosen "guides us in the selection
of vocabulary and activities that include continual brainswitching...For example, ['classical'] TPR, storytelling by the instructor,
and dramatic skits created by students are techniques that play
to the right brain while speaking, reading, and writing mini-dia-
logues and stories play to the left brain." (Asher, 1996: page 3-
56) (Singing and drawing are other right-brain activities; grammar exercises and questions to answer in writing are left-brain
activities.) Brainswitching would only begin after speech by students has begun to emerge.

This book is loaded with other types of TPR activities which
you can use, both right-brain and left-brain. Also, Ramiro
García's *Instructor's Notebook: How to Apply TPR for Best Results* (1988) and *The Graphics Book* (1991) provide lots of very
good variations, and so do Stephen Mark "Gil" Silvers' *Command
Book* (1988) and *Listen and Perform* (1985). You will have to ex-
periment to find out how much "classical" TPR works along with
how much of this or that.

Much of the solution to adaptation and other problems lies in
the way the teacher handles things. TPR Storytelling appears to
avoid it virtually completely through continual variation of activities and through high-interest content. Read Chapter 4 for details on how this is accomplished.

> TIP: No matter what activities your class is doing, but es-
> pecially if they're doing TPR activities, make sure there
> is adequate ventilation. A stuffy room can make what
> would otherwise be a very fruitful and scintillating activ-
> ity into a very unpleasant one.

Classroom Management

There can be another reason why you would sometimes want to vary the type of activity your class engages in. Emotional involvement along with physical involvement often leads to considerable excitement. Full body action is likely to be more exciting than actions done with the hands (for more on "hand TPR," see pp. 44-49). You may want your class to respond with full body movements at times, with hand movements at others. Taking into account the ages and maturity of a class, you will want to choose the type of activity that follows the excitement. The degree of the excitement engendered by the activity and the special character of it should be noticed. Be aware too that some TPR activities are more exciting (inciting?) than others. Some students, and some groups, will revel in the excitement with no negative effects throughout a whole class period. Others (depending on age and maturity) will get overly excited, so you will want to have them do something quiet to calm them down. Numerous factors can affect the mood of a class, so that what is just fine one day may be too exciting another. There's springtime, of course, and puberty and love and family problems and so on and so forth.

Discipline, then, can be a problem. Blaine Ray, the creator of TPR Storytelling who teaches Spanish at Stockdale High School in Bakersfield, California, has some suggestions to avoid discipline problems in many classrooms:

- Students must speak only the target language. (The teacher may speak the students' first language when deemed necessary.)
- Students must perform the actions.
- Students must stay on task when they're in pairs or small groups.

When they fail to do any of these things, they are penalized by paying points, points which they can make up in some other way. Ray allows them to "take the day off" at the cost of 10% of their participation grade. When he notices someone sloughing off, he asks if they would like to take the day off. Nearly always they say no and get with it immediately.

When Students Are Not Performing as Well as You Think They Should Be

There are various possible remedies. Some ideas:

1. Backtrack and do some enabling activities, activities that will prepare them well to do what they're not doing well. It pays to think ahead about what to do if the need arises.

2. Change activities; get them to brainswitch by trying a completely different type of activity. Do something calm rather than active or vice versa.

3. Open a window or door to improve ventilation.

TPR Presenters and Sources of TPR Materials

PRESENTERS

This is a partial list of teachers who give workshops on TPR. It is a slightly expanded version of the one given on pp. 3-72 and 3-73 of Asher's book *Learning Another Language Through Actions* (1996). Immediately following it is a list of teachers who give workshops on TPR Storytelling as well as TPR.

Tam Agosti-Gisler
Teachables-n-Touchables
200 West 34th Ave.,
 Suite 670
Anchorage, AK 99503
Phone: (907) 272-9227

Kathryn J. Akiyama Kim
Watermelon School
Yuksam-dong 833-2
Sungbo-Yuksam Bldg.,
 2nd Floor
Kangnam-ku
Seoul, Korea
Phone: (2) 564 8091
Fax: (2) 564-8093

Christine Anderson
P.O. Box 9064
Scottsdale, AZ 85252
Phone: (800) TPR IS FUN
Phone: (602) 582-5543

Anne Arruda
Teachables-n-Touchables
200 West 34th Ave.,
 Suite 670
Anchorage, AK 99503
Phone: (907) 344-1462

Dr. James J. Asher
P.O. Box 1102
Los Gatos, CA 95031
Phone: (408) 395-7600
Fax: (408) 395-8440
TPR World@aol.com
www.tpr-world.com

Dr. Francisco Cabello
Dept. of Modern Language
Southern Oregon State College
Ashland, OR 97520
Phone: (503) 552-6435
Fax: (503) 482-6429

Dr. Barbara Carvill
Department of German
Calvin College
Grand Rapids, MI 49506
Phone: (616) 957-6365

Berty Segal Cook
749 Eucalyptus St.
Brea, CA 92621
Phone: (714) 529-5359
Fax: (714) 529-3882
BertySegal@aol.com
www.agoralang.com/tpr-
 bertysegal.html

Elizabeth Cunniff
Language Laboratory
Indiana University at
 South Bend
1700 Mishawaka Ave.
South Bend, IN 46634

Bill Denevan
105 Lance Court
Santa Cruz, CA 95065
Phone: (408) 459-6894

Marge Dequine
130 El Monte Ct.
Los Altos, CA 94022
Phone: (415) 948-6183

Joan Eling
Mountlake Terrace
  High School
21801 44th Ave. West
Mountlake Terrace, WA 98043
Phone: (206) 670-7776

Ramiro García
5161 Cordoy Lane
San Jose, CA 95124
Phone: (408) 267-0451

Joanne "Jody" Klopp
3513 N. W. 16th St.
Oklahoma City, OK 73107
Phone: (405) 947-3906

Professor Morio Kohno
5-6-13 Kaminotani, Sumaku
Kobe 654-01
Japan

Dr. Gen Lennon
8420 Cornell Ave.
St. Louis, MO 63132
Phone: (314) 997-0845

Gene Lynch
1317 E. Oak
Lompoc, CA 93436
Phone: (805) 736-8889

Joe Moore
44 Morningside Drive
Tiffin, OH 44883
Phone: (419) 447-2756

Mary Sisk Noguchi
410 Nisshin Park Mansion
1-103 Sakae, Nisshin-cho
Aichi-gun, Aichi-ken
Japan 470-01
Phone: 05617-2-2006

Jo Ann Olliphant
11004 111th St. S.W.
Tacoma, WA 98498
Phone: (206) 584-7473

Kay Price
75 No. El Monte Ave.
Los Altos, CA 94022
Phone: (415) 948-2051

John Proudian
5658 North Sherman Ave.
Fresno, CA 93710
Phone: (209) 439-1797

Berty Segal
(see Berty Segal Cook)

Dr. Sam L. Slick, Chairman
Department of Foreign
  Languages
University of Southern
  Mississippi
P.O. Box 5038
Hattiesburg, MS 39406
Phone: (601) 266-4964

Carol Spady
Memorial Middle School
S. Portland School Depart-
  ment
130 Westcott Road
S. Portland, ME 04106
Phone: (207) 761-8330

Professor Tadashi Takahashi
Supervisor of English Educa-
  tion
Himeji City Board of Education
1165-2, Shikata, Kakogawa
Hyogo 675-03
Japan
Phone: 0794-52-2424

Dr. David Wolfe
7021 Chew Ave.
Philadelphia, PA 19119
Phone: (215) 248-2582

Laura Zink de Días
22713 Lakeview Drive, B-5
Mountlake Terrace, WA 98043

TPR Storytelling Presenters

Melinda Forward
PO Box 21847
Albuquerque, NM 87154-1847
Toll-free phone and fax:
 (866) 750-1181
mforward@eaze.net
www.melindaforward.com

Carol Gaab
1642 West Butler Drive
Chandler, AZ 85224
(800) 958-5552
Phone and fax:
 (602) 963-3463
Gaab5@aol.com
www.tprstorytelling.com

Susan Gross
515 Pluto Dr.
Colorado Springs, CO 80906
(719) 471-0041
s_gross@compuserve.com

Gale Mackey
10105 Sunset Canyon Drive
Bakersfield, CA 93311
Phone: (805) 665-8135
Cuentista@aol.com

Valeri Marsh
P.O. Box 9064
Scottsdale, AZ 85252
(800) TPR IS FUN =
 (800) 877-4738
Fax: (602) 808-8744
TPRISFUN@aol.com
www.tprstorytelling.com

Joe Neilson
5418 E. 9th St.
Tucson, AZ 85711
Phone: (520) 745-5140
jrnombligo@aol.com

Shirley Ogle
2536 Twin Buttes Dr. NE
Rio Rancho, NM 87124
Phone: 505 867-6049
John-Shirley-Ogle@worldnet.
 att.net
http://home.switchboard.com/
 ShirleyOgleTPRStorytelling
 Plus

Blaine Ray
Blaine Ray Workshops
3820 Amur Maple Drive
Bakersfield, CA 93311
Toll-free phone: (888) 373-1920
Fax: (661) 665-8071
BlaineRay@aol.com
www.BlainerayTPRS.com

Lynn Rogers
502 E. Andrew
Springdale, AR 72764

Contee Seely
Command Performance
 Language Institute
1755 Hopkins Street
Berkeley, CA 94707-2714
Phone and fax:
 (510) 524-1191
consee@aol.com

MAJOR SOURCES OF TPR MATERIALS

Sky Oaks Productions
P.O. Box 1102
Los Gatos, CA 95031
(408) 395-7600
Fax (408) 395-8440
TPR World@aol.com
www.tpr-world.com

Berty Segal, Inc.
1749 Eucalyptus St.
Brea, CA 92821
(714) 529-5359
Fax (714) 529-3882
BertySegal@aol.com
www.tprsource.com

Spanish, French, German &
Teachers' Resources:

Teacher's Discovery
2741 Paldan Dr.
Auburn Hills, MI 48326
(800) 832-2437
Fax (248) 340-7212
www.teachersdiscovery.com

ESL, Spanish & Teachers'
Resources:

Alta Book Center
14 Adrian Court
Burlingame, CA 94010
(415) 692-1285
(800) ALTA/ESL
Fax (415) 692-4654
Fax (800) ALTA/FAX
altaesl@aol.com

All the distributors listed on the final page also carry TPR items.

SOURCES OF TPR STORYTELLING MATERIALS

Below are the names and contact information of organizations and individuals which have TPR Storytelling materials available:

Alta Book Center
See the final page of this book.

Berty Segal, Inc.
See the final page of this book.

Blaine Ray Workshops
3820 Amur Maple Drive
Bakersfield, CA 93311
Phone: (805) 665-9523
Fax: (805) 665-8071
BlaineRay@aol.com
www.BlainerayTPRS.com

C.W. Publishing
P.O. Box 9064
Scottsdale, AZ 85252
(800) TPR IS FUN =
    (800) 877-4738
Fax: (602) 963-3463
TPRISFUN@aol.com
www.tprstorytelling.com

TPR Storytelling Plus
Melinda Forward
PO Box 21847
Albuquerque, NM 87154-1847
Toll-free phone and fax:
    (866) 750-1181
mforward@eaze.net
www.melindaforward.com

TPR Storytelling Plus
Shirley Ogle
2536 Twin Buttes Dr. NE
Rio Rancho, NM 87124
Phone: 505 867-6049
John-Shirley-Ogle@worldnet.
    att.net
http://home.switchboard.com/
    ShirleyOgleTPRStorytelling
    Plus

Gessler Publishing
See the final page of this book.

Sky Oaks Productions
See above.

Teacher's Discovery
See above.

Some of the other Command Performance Language Institute distributors listed on the last page also carry selected titles. Just ask.

References and Bibliography

REFERENCES

Asher, James J. 1972. Children's first language as a model for second language learning. *The Modern Language Journal 56*, 3: 133-139.

Asher, James J. 1981. The extinction of second language learning in American schools: an intervention model. *The Comprehension Approach to Foreign Language Instruction. H.* Winitz (ed.). Rowley, MA: Newbury House.

Asher, James J. 1988. *Brainswitching*. Los Gatos, CA: Sky Oaks.

Asher, James J. 1996. *Learning Another Language Through Actions: The Complete Teacher's Guidebook*. 5th ed. Los Gatos, CA: Sky Oaks.

Asher, James J. 1995. *The Super School*. Los Gatos, CA: Sky Oaks Productions.

Benson, Valerie A. 1994. Harold E. Palmer: A Pioneer of English Language Teaching. *Bulletin of The Suzugamine Women's College Cultural and Social Science Studies 41*, December: 79-93.

Burling, Robbins. 1982. *Sounding Right*. Rowley, MA: Newbury House.

Butterworth, Rod and Mickey Flodin. 1983, 1991. *The Perigree Visual Dictionary of Signing*. New York: Putnam. Over 1,250 signs of American Sign Language.

Cabello, Francisco. 1985. *Total Physical Response in First Year Spanish*. Los Gatos, CA: Sky Oaks. (also available in English and French)

Draper, Jamie B. 1991. *Foreign Language Enrollments in Public Secondary Schools, Fall 1989 and Fall 1990*. Yonkers, NY: ACTFL (American Council on the Teaching of Foreign Languages).

Forward, Melinda and Shirley Ogle. 1997a. *Organizing and Managing a TPR Storytelling Classroom*. Fort Worth, TX: TPR Storytelling Plus.

Forward, Melinda and Shirley Ogle. 1997b. *TPR Storytelling Activities*. Fort Worth, TX: TPR Storytelling Plus.

Forward, Melinda and Shirley Ogle. 1997-98 *Getting Started in TPR Storytelling Plus*. Fort Worth, TX: TPR Storytelling Plus. (A series of 9 chapters for each of French, Spanish and ESL; about half available as this book goes to press; available chapter by chapter; teacher's manuals available.)

Fukuda, Kazue, Mary Sisk Noguchi, Contee Seely and Elizabeth Romijn. 1994. *Iki Iki Nihongo: Live Action Japanese*. Berkeley, CA: Command Performance.

Gaab, Carol. 1998. *Spanish K-2 TPR Storytelling Curriculum* (tentative title). Scottsdale, Arizona: C.W. Publishing.

Galvan, Mary. 1979-80. Directed apparently unpublished research on the frequency of imperatives in on-the-job language. Austin, Texas: Resource Development Institute.

García, Ramiro. 1988. *Instructor's Notebook: How to Apply TPR for Best Results*. 2nd ed. Los Gatos, CA: Sky Oaks.

García, Ramiro. 1991. *The Graphics Book*. Los Gatos, CA: Sky Oaks. (available in English, Spanish, French, German)

Gouin, François. 1880. *L'art d'enseigner et d'étudier les langues*. Paris: Librairie Fischbacher. (English translation by H. Swan and V. Bétis: 1892. *The Art of Teaching and Studying Languages*. London: Philip.)

Griffee, Dale T. 1981. A new look at Total Physical Response. *Cross Currents 8*, 2: 43-49.

Griffee, Dale T. 1982. *Listen and Act*. Tokyo and Tucson: Lingual House.

Henrichsen, Lynn Earl. 1989. *Diffusion of Innovations in English Language Teaching*. Westport, CT: Greenwood Press.

Katz, Pamela and Laurie Nesrala. Date unknown. Spanish chart. *The Verb Wall*. Available from Pam Katz at Halton High School, Forth Worth, Texas.

Kalivoda, Theodore B., Gennelle Morain and Robert J. Elkins. 1971. The Audio-Motor Unit: a listening comprehension strategy that works. *Foreign Language Annals 4*, 392-400.

Kelly, Louis G. 1969. *25 Centuries of Language Teaching*. Rowley, MA: Newbury House.

Klopp, Joanne R. 1989. *Actionlogues*. Los Gatos, CA: Sky Oaks. (available in Spanish, French, German; see p. 174)

Krashen, Stephen D. 1981. The "fundamental pedagogical principle" in second language teaching. *Studia Linguistica 35*, 1-2: 50-70.

Krashen, Stephen D. and Tracy D. Terrell. 1983. *The Natural Approach*. Hayward, CA: Alemany Press. Currently available from Tappan, NJ: Prentice-Hall.

Lawson, John H. 1971. Should foreign language be eliminated from the curriculum? In J.W. Dodge (ed.), *The Case For Foreign Language Study*. New York: Modern Language Association Materials Center.

Loftus, Elizabeth. 1980. *Memory: Surprising New Insights Into How We Remember and Why We Forget*. Reading, MA: Addison-Wesley.

MacGowan-Gilhooly, Adele. 1993. *Achieving Fluency in English*. 2nd ed. Dubuque, IA: Kendall/Hunt.

MacGowan-Gilhooly, Adele. 1995. *Achieving Clarity in English*. 2nd ed. Dubuque, IA: Kendall/Hunt.

Mackey, Gale. 1996. *¡Mírame, puedo cantar!—Nivel 2*. Audio cassette. Also lyrics and exercise book (with Contee Seely, 1997). Berkeley, CA: Command Performance.

Mackey, Gale. 1997a. *¡Mírame, puedo cantar!—Nivel 1*. Audio cassette. Bakersfield, CA: Blaine Ray Workshops and Berkeley, CA: Command Performance.

Mackey, Gale. 1997b. *Spanish Grammar Songs*. Bakersfield, CA: Blaine Ray Workshops and Berkeley, CA: Command Performance.

Marsh, Valeri (a.k.a. Valeri Waxman-Marsh) and Christine Anderson. 1994. *¡Cuéntame! TPR Storytelling: An Introductory Spanish Course for Elementary School Students*. 2nd ed. Scottsdale, Arizona: C.W. Publishing. (teacher's manual, overhead transparencies, blackline masters and test packet (the last 3 by Carol Gaab) also available)

Marsh, Valeri (a.k.a. Valeri Waxman-Marsh) and Christine Anderson. 1994. *¡Cuéntame más!: TPR Storytelling: An Introductory Spanish Course for Middle School Students*. 2nd ed. Scottsdale, Arizona: C.W. Publishing. (teacher's manual also available)

Marsh, Valeri (a.k.a. Valeri Waxman-Marsh) and Christine Anderson. *Raconte-moi!: TPR Storytelling: An Introductory French Course for Elementary School Students*, 1994, 1995. Scottsdale, Arizona: C.W. Publishing. (teacher's manual also available)

Marsh, Valeri (a.k.a. Valeri Waxman-Marsh) and Christine Anderson. *Raconte-moi encore!: TPR Storytelling: An Introductory French Course for Middle School Students*, 1994, 1995. Scottsdale, Arizona: C.W. Publishing. (teacher's manual also available)

Marsh, Valeri (a.k.a. Valeri Waxman-Marsh) and Christine Anderson. ESL adaptation by Carol Gaab. *Tell Me More!: TPR Storytelling: An Introductory ESL Course for Middle School Students*, 1998. Scottsdale, Arizona: C.W. Publishing. (teacher's manual, overhead transparencies, blackline masters and test packet also available)

Nelson, Gayle and Thomas Winters. 1993. *Operations in English*. Brattleboro, VT: Pro Lingua. (see p. 174)

Neilson, Joe and Blaine Ray. 1996. *Mini-stories for Look, I Can Talk!* Bakersfield, CA: Blaine Ray Workshops. (available in English, Spanish and French (1997))

Noguchi, Mary Sisk. 1995. Iki Iki Nihongo: Teaching Japanese grammar patterns with TPR action sequences. *The Meijo-Shogaku 44*, February: 1-34.

Ogle, Shirley. 1997. *The Spanish Verb Timeline*. Verb wall charts. Fort Worth, TX: TPR Storytelling Plus.

Palmer, Harold and Dorothée Palmer. 1925. *English through Actions*. Tokyo: Kaitakusha. (Reissued in 1955. Slightly revised later edition: 1959. London: Longman.)

Piaget, Jean. 1955. *The Construction of Reality in the Child*. New York: Basic Books.

Pimsleur, Paul. 1980. *How to Learn a Foreign Language*. Boston: Heinle & Heinle.

Ray, Blaine. 1990. *Look, I Can Talk!* Los Gatos, CA: Sky Oaks. (available in English, Spanish, French, German; overhead transparencies also available)

Ray, Blaine. 1995. *TPR Storytelling Video*. Bakersfield, CA: Blaine Ray Workshops and Berkeley, CA: Command Performance.

Ray, Blaine. 1996a. *Mini-stories for **Look, I Can Talk More!*** Bakersfield, CA: Blaine Ray Workshops. (currently available only in English; English version can be adapted for Spanish and French)

Ray, Blaine. 1996b. *Mini-stories for **Look, I'm Still Talking!*** Bakersfield, CA: Blaine Ray Workshops. (currently available only in English; English version can be adapted for Spanish and French)

Ray, Blaine. 1998. *Look, I Can Talk! Teacher's Guidebook.* 3rd ed. (for Spanish, French, German and English) Los Gatos, CA: Sky Oaks.

Ray, Blaine. 2001. *New Blaine Ray TPR Storytelling Workshop Video.* Produced by Walter Nagel. Akron, OH: Natcom Productions.

Ray, Blaine, Joe Neilson, Dave Cline and Carole Stevens. 1992. *Look, I Can Talk More!* Los Gatos, CA: Sky Oaks. (available in English, Spanish, French; overhead transparencies also available)

Ray, Blaine and Joe Neilson. *Look, I'm Still Talking!* 1993. Originally published by the authors; now published by: Berkeley, CA: Command Performance. (available in English, Spanish and French; obtainable Blaine Ray Workshops and from many distributors listed on final page.)

Ray, Blaine and Contee Seely. 1998. *Fluency Through TPR Storytelling.* 2nd ed. Berkeley, CA: Command Performance.

Romijn, Elizabeth and Contee Seely. 1997. *Live Action English.* Millennium edition. Berkeley, CA: Command Performance. (available in English, French, Spanish, German, Italian and Japanese; co-authors for Japanese version: Kazue Fukuda and Mary Sisk Noguchi)

Rosen, Joan M. 1994. *TPR Student Kit Stories.* Los Gatos, CA: Sky Oaks. (based on Asher's TPR student kits; available in English only)

Schessler, Eric J. 1984. *English Grammar Through Actions.* Los Gatos, CA: Sky Oaks. (also available in Spanish and French)

Seely, Contee. 1982. Total Physical Response is More Than Commands—At All Levels. *Cross Currents 9*, 2: 45-65.

Seely, Contee. forthcoming. *¡Español con impacto!: TPR Spanish with Fluency.* 7th ed. Berkeley, CA: Command Performance. (basic Spanish through TPR and TPR Storytelling)

Segal, Bertha E. 1992. *Teaching English Through Action.* Brea, CA: Berty Segal, Inc. (available in Spanish, French, German, Japanese, Russian, Secwepemc, Iñupiak and St´at'imcets)

Shapiro, Norma and Carol Genser. 1994. *Chalk Talks.* Berkeley, CA: Command Performance.

Silvers, Stephen M. 1988. *The Command Book.* Los Gatos, CA: Sky Oaks.

Silvers, Stephen M. 1985. *Listen and Perform.* Los Gatos, CA: Sky Oaks. (available in English, Spanish and French)

Sternberg, Martin L.A. 1981, 1987. *American Sign Language Dictionary.* New York: Harper & Row.

Terrell, Tracy D., Magdalena Andrade, Jeanne Egasse and Elías Miguel Muñoz. 1990. *Dos mundos.* 2nd ed. (1994: 3rd ed.) New York: McGraw-Hill.

Terrell, Tracy D., Mary B. Rogers, Betsy K. Barnes and Marguerite Wolff-Hessini. 1993. *Deux mondes.* 2nd ed. New York: McGraw-Hill.

Terrell, Tracy D., Erwin Tschirner, Brigitte Nikolai and Herbert Genzmer. 1995. *Kontakte.* 3rd ed. New York: McGraw-Hill.

Turner, Lisa Ray and Blaine Ray. 1998. *Casi se muere.* Berkeley, CA: Command Performance.

BIBLIOGRAPHY OF OTHER TPR WORKS

Action Series Books

Live Action English, *¡Viva la acción!: Live Action Spanish*, *Vive l'action!: Live Action French*, *Lernt aktiv!: Live Action German*, *Viva l'azione!: Live Action Italian* and *Iki Iki Nihongo: Live Action Japanese*, by Elizabeth Romijn and Contee Seely (with Kazue Fukuda and Mary Sisk Noguchi for Japanese version) (Berkeley, CA: Command Performance, 1997, 1989, 1989, 1991, 1993, 1994), contain 67 to 70 lessons like those on pp. 18 and 22 of this book.

Action English Pictures, with illustrations by former English student Noriko Takahashi and text by Maxine Frauman-Prickel (Hayward, CA: Alemany Press, 1985), is based directly on *Live Action English*. It consists of 66 duplicatable picture lessons — 32 or more of which are the very same series which are in the *Live Action* books above, but without words. There is a picture for each line of text in the lessons from the *Live Action* books. (Currently available from Alta Book Center—see the final page.)

The Children's Response by Caroline Linse (Hayward, CA: Alemany Press, 1983) is 60 English series deftly designed for elementary school children. (Temporarily out of print.)

Actionlogues by Joanne "Jody" Klopp (Los Gatos, CA: Sky Oaks Productions, 1985; see final page or p. 166) presents 25 series with a photograph for each line — available in Spanish, French and German only; cassettes available in all three languages.

Action Sequence Stories by Constance Williams (Menlo Park, CA: Williams and Williams, 1987 and 1988; currently available from Ballard & Tighe, 480 Atlas St., Brea, CA 92621 (phone: (800) 321-4322)) consists of 2 kits of materials, each of which includes 50 six-line command sequences. Chinese, English, Spanish, French, Italian and German versions of the sequences are available.

Operations in English by Gayle Nelson and Thomas Winters (Brattleboro, VT: Pro Lingua, 1993; phone: (800) 366-4775) has 55 everyday sequences in English. This is a revised and expanded edition of *ESL Operations*, published by Newbury House in 1980.

Picture It!: Sequences for Conversation (Tokyo: International Communications, 1978; New York: Regents, 1981) has 60 eight-line, fully-illustrated sequences which are in a variety of English tenses and were not intended to be acted out. While only a handful are in the imperative, all can be done with action and adapted to the imperative. (Currently available from Prentice Hall Regents; phone: 800-947-7700; fax: 515-284-2607.)

Listen and Act by Dale Griffee (Tokyo and Tucson; Lingual House, 1982) contains "mini-drama" sequences in which a "director" gives commands to "actors" and "actresses" who perform the actions. It is out of print.

Publications of Sky Oaks Productions
(in addition to those mentioned in the references on pp. 168-173 above) (see address, etc., on the final page or p. 166)

García, Ramiro. *TPR Bingo* (available in English, Spanish, French, German)

Márquez, Nancy. *Learning With Movements: TPR English.* For elementary school. (Beginners) (also available in Spanish and French)

Ray, Blaine. *Look, I Can Talk!* (Level 1) (Student Book) (available in English, Spanish, French, German)

Ray, Blaine. *Look, I Can Talk! Teacher's Guidebook.* (for all languages)

Ray, Blaine, Joe Neilson, Dave Cline and Carole Stevens. *Look, I Can Talk, More!* (Level 2) (Student Book) (available in English, Spanish, French)

Woodruff-Wieding, M. and L.J. Ayala. *Favorite Games for FL-ESL Classes.* TPR and other active games.

Woodruff, Margaret. *Comprehension-Based Language Lessons.* Basic text for the first 60 hours. (available in German & English)

James J. Asher's TPR Student Kits are available in English, Spanish, French and German on the following topics:

Farm, Harbor, Firestation—Dial 911, Fun In The Snow, Gas Station, Home, Kitchen, Town, Airport, Department Store, Hospital, Classroom, United States Map, European Map, Country Garden, Main Street, Supermarket, Playground, Beach, Picnic, Restaurant, Calendar; 4-in-One: Community, School, Work, Leisure; and (in English only) World Map.

James J. Asher's TPR Teacher Kits:

Home, Kitchen, Town, Airport.

Videos produced by James J. Asher:

Children Learning Another Language: An Innovative Approach
A Motivational Strategy for Language Learning
Strategy for Second Language Learning
Demonstration of a New Strategy in Language Learning

Publications of Berty Segal, Inc.

(in addition to those mentioned in the references on pp. 168-173 above) (see address, etc., on the final page or p. 166)

François, Linda. *English in Action for Adults and Teens.*

Raileanu, Lia. *Le français par l'intermédiaire de la Réponse Physique Totale.* (French teacher and student text)

Raileanu, Lia. *Tanoshii Nihongo through TPR.* (Japanese teacher and student text)

Segal, Bertha. *Part 2: Teaching English...Speaking, Reading, Writing.* (available for foreign language teaching also, with a special supplement)

Segal, Bertha. *Teaching English Through Action.* 102 lesson plans. (available in English, Spanish, French, German, Japanese, Russian, Secwepemc, Iñupiak and St´at'imcets)

Segal, Bertha. *We Learn English Through Action.* Student book. (available in English, Spanish, French and German)

Videos available from Berty Segal, Inc.:

TPR/Natural Approach Classrooms (for teacher training)
TPR/Accelerated Learning (Spanish, French, German or Italian) (for students)

176

A Few More Items
(several of which are available from Sky Oaks, Berty Segal, Inc. and some of the other distributors on the final page)

Blaine Ray. *Teaching Grammar Communicatively.* New York and Roanoke, VA: Gessler Publishing.

Galloway, Vicki, Dorothy Joba and Angela Labarca. *¡Acción!,* Levels 1 and 2. Mission Hills, CA: Glencoe. Spanish high school series with lots of TPR.

May, Laurie and Kaoru Kimura. *Live Japanese!* (forthcoming) Written especially for middle school classes, this book contains student and teacher materials for Japanese through TPR and TPR Storytelling. Available from Ms. May at 5413 Willowmere Way, Baltimore, MD 21212; phone: (410) 435-8864; fax: (410) 296-2538; e-mail: lmay@stpauls.pvt.k12.md.us.

Olliphant, Jo Ann. *Total Physical Fun.* Tacoma, WA: Sahmarsh Publishing (11004 111th St. S.W., Tacoma, WA 98498; phone: 206-584-7473). A great variety of cooperative TPR and other playful activities and strategies for all levels and languages.

Payne, Judith. *Involve Me and I'll Learn.* CA: JP Enterprises (P.O. Box 927, Loomis, CA 95650). A guide to first level instruction, with vocabulary in English, Spanish, French and German.

Price, Kay and Marge Dequine. Quick Start in English Program. Los Altos, CA: Quick Start in English (75 N. El Monte Ave., Los Altos, CA 94022; phone: 415-948-2051). Many components for ESL for preschool through adult levels, including texts, tests, pictures, transparencies, readers, games, songs, teacher's guide, etc.

Shioiri-Clark, Yoko. *Japanese in Action* (tentative title). New York: McGraw-Hill. (forthcoming) First-year college and high school text with much TPR and TPR Storytelling.

Wachman, Robert C. "Beginning Effectively With TPR." International Catholic Migration Commission, the Philippines. Teacher training video. Now available from the producer at Yuba College, 2088 N. Beale Rd., Marysville, CA 95901; phone: 916-674-8185; e-mail: RWachman@aol.com.

THE AUTHORS

Contee Seely graduated from Princeton University in 1961. He has taught English to adult speakers of other languages in Ecuador, Peru, Chile and the United States and has also taught Spanish in high school and to adults (including Peace Corps trainees) in the U.S. and at Vista College in Berkeley. He is the author of *¡Español con impacto!: TPR Spanish with Fluency* (out of print at this time but being revised). With Elizabeth Kuizenga Romijn he is co-author of the *Live Action* series of books in English, French, Spanish, German, Italian and (also with Kazue Fukuda and Mary Sisk Noguchi) Japanese. With Elizabeth Kuizenga Romijn, Larry Statan, Elizabeth Hanson-Smith and Robert Wachman, he created the CD-ROM *Live Action English Interactive*. Currently he teaches Spanish for Neighborhood Centers Adult School in the Oakland public schools in the evening. In 1989 he received the Excellence in Teaching Award presented by the California Council for Adult Education. He is publisher at the Command Performance Language Institute in Berkeley. He and his wife of 34 years, Maggie, live in Berkeley and have a son, Michael, and a daughter, Christina.

Elizabeth Kuizenga Romijn grew up in Ann Arbor, Michigan. She received a B.A. in Linguistics from the University of California in Berkeley in 1969 and began teaching ESL that fall for the Mission Campus of City College of San Francisco, where she is still teaching today, specializing in lower levels and ESL Literacy. In 1983 she received an M.A. in Linguistics-ESL from San Jose State University. She is the author of *Puppies or Poppies? ESL Bingo* (see next page). With Contee Seely she is co-author of the *Live Action* series of books in English, French, Spanish, German, Italian and (also with Kazue Fukuda and Mary Sisk Noguchi) Japanese. With Contee Seely, Larry Statan, Elizabeth Hanson-Smith and Robert Wachman, she created the CD-ROM *Live Action English Interactive*. She has presented teacher workshops on TPR and multi-level ESL thruout California. She has two daughters, Rebecca Romijn-Stamos and Tamara Romijn, and lives in Richmond, California.

FLUENCY THROUGH TPR STORYTELLING:
Achieving Real Language Acquisition in School
2nd or 3rd Edition
Blaine Ray & Contee Seely

The definitive treatment of TPR Storytelling by the originator, Blaine Ray, and Contee Seely. TPR is used to teach vocabulary from day one throughout four years. Many other effective techniques come into play at various stages. After 15 to 30 class hours, storytelling begins. Within 10 to 20 more hours, students are speaking the target language without ever having memorized anything, and their fluency is developing daily. Teachers love what their students can do. Students do too. This book shows how to keep students acquiring with fascination at every level. Beware! It may change your expectations of what students can accomplish in the classroom and make language teaching more exciting and fulfilling than ever.

LIVE ACTION ENGLISH INTERACTIVE
TPR on a Computer!
[AVAILABLE for WINDOWS and MACINTOSH]
content by Elizabeth Kuizenga Romijn and Contee Seely; created by Larry Statan; CALL consultants: Elizabeth Hanson-Smith and Robert Wachman

The first Total Physical Response computer program ever. Based on the classic TPR text *Live Action English* by Romijn and Seely (below). Practical vocabulary in context through video and still photos in 12 action sequences. Innovative interactive TPR exercises. Verb form practice in context in 4 essential tenses. Dictations, help, more. High beginning, low intermediate. Grades 4-12, college, adult levels. See the DEMO at http://www.speakware.com. Dynamic! Effective! Captivating!

Live Action English - Millennium (3rd) Edition
Elizabeth Kuizenga Romijn and Contee Seely

The book that shouts out: "Hey! This is fun! Let's do it!" Over 50,000 copies sold world-wide! The first student/teacher book based on James J. Asher's Total Physical Response (TPR). 67 lively "happenings" (illustrated series of commands) for students of all ages in beginning, intermediate and multilevel classes. Much practical colloquial language not found in other texts. Thorough teacher's guide included. Foreword by Asher.

Puppies or Poppies? ESL Bingo
Elizabeth Kuizenga Romijn

Listening exercises in the form of bingo games! Students love to play bingo. Over 65 bingo games that reinforce numerous classic ESL language points. For children and adults, from beginning ESL literacy levels thru high intermediate ESL. Each game focuses on •a vocabulary topic •a grammar point or •a tricky sound discrimination. Detailed instructions, reproducible student materials, calling cards for games.

ALL ITEMS AVAILABLE FROM DISTRIBUTORS ON LAST PAGE

DISTRIBUTORS

of Command Performance Language Institute materials

Midwest European
Publications
915 Foster St.
Evanston, IL 60201-3199
(847) 866-6289
(800) 380-8919
Fax (847) 866-6290
info@mep-eli.com
www.mep-eli.com

Miller Educational
Materials
P.O. Box 2428
Buena Park, CA 90621
(800) MEM 4 ESL
Toll Free Fax (888) 462-0042
MillerEdu@aol.com
www.millereducational.
com

Tempo Bookstore
4905 Wisconsin Ave., N.W.
Washington, DC 20016
(202) 363-6683
Fax (202) 363-6686
Tempobookstore@usa.net

Multi-Cultural Books
& Videos
28880 Southfield Rd.,
Suite 183
Lathrup Village, MI 48076
(248) 559-2676
(800) 567-2220
Fax (248) 559-2465
service@multiculbv.com
www.multiculbv.com

World of Reading, Ltd.
P.O. Box 13092
Atlanta, GA 30324-0092
(404) 233-4042
(800) 729-3703
Fax (404) 237-5511
polyglot@wor.com
www.wor.com

Continental Book Co.
80-00 Cooper Ave. #29
Glendale, NY 11385
(718) 326-0560
Fax (718) 326-4276
www.continentalbook.
com

Carlex
P.O. Box 81786
Rochester, MI 48308-1786
(800) 526-3768
Fax (248) 852-7142
www.carlexonline.com

Berty Segal, Inc.
1749 E. Eucalyptus St.
Brea, CA 92821
(714) 529-5359
Fax (714) 529-3882
BertySegal@aol.com
www.tprsource.com

Entry Publishing
& Consulting
P.O. Box 20277
New York, NY 10025
(212) 662-9703
Toll Free (888) 601-9860
Fax: (212) 662-0549

The English Resource
15-15-2F Matsugae-cho
Sagamihara-shi,
Kanagawa-ken
JAPAN 228
Tel 042-744-8898
Fax 042-744-8897
resource@twics.com

Calliope Books
Route 3, Box 3395
Saylorsburg, PA 18353
Tel/Fax (610) 381-2587

International Book Centre
2391 Auburn Rd.
Shelby Township, MI 48317
(810) 879-8436
Fax (810) 254-7230

Edumate
2231 Morena Blvd.
San Diego, CA 92110
(619) 275-7117
Fax (619) 275-7120
GusBla@aol.com

Authors & Editors
10736 Jefferson Blvd. #104
Culver City, CA 90230
(310) 836-2014

Canadian Resources for
ESL
15 Ravina Crescent
Toronto, Ontario
CANADA M4J 3L9
(416) 466-7875
Fax (416) 466-4383
Thane@interlog.com
www.interlog.com/
~thane

Alta Book Center
14 Adrian Court
Burlingame, CA 94010
(650) 692-1285
(800) ALTAESL
Fax (650) 692-4654
Fax (800) ALTAFAX
info@altaesl.com
www.altaesl.com

European Book Co.
925 Larkin St.
San Francisco, CA 94109
(415) 474-0626

Delta Systems, Inc.
1400 Miller Parkway
McHenry, IL 60050
(815) 36- DELTA
(800) 323-8270
Fax (800) 909-9901
custsvc@delta-systems.
com
www.delta-systems.
com

Educational Showcase
3519 E. Ten Mile Rd.
Warren, MI 48091
(810) 758-3013
(800) 213-3671
Fax (810) 756-2016

BookLink
465 Broad Ave.
Leonia, NJ 07605
(201) 947-3471
Fax (201) 947-6321
booklink@intac.com

David English House
6F Seojung Bldg.
1308-14 Seocho 4 Dong
Seocho-dong
Seoul 137-074
KOREA
Tel 02)594-7625
Fax 02)591-7626
hkhwang1@chollian.
net
www.eltkorea.com

Continental Book Co.
625 E. 70th Ave., Unit 5
Denver, CO 80229
(303) 289-1761
Fax (800) 279-1764
esl@continentalbook.
com
www.continentalbook.
com

Sky Oaks Productions
P.O. Box 1102
Los Gatos, CA 95031
(408) 395-7600
Fax (408) 395-8440
TPR World@aol.com
www.tpr-world.com

Multi-Cultural Books
& Videos
12033 St. Thomas Crescent
Tecumseh, ONT
CANADA N 8N 3V6
(519) 735-3313
Fax (519) 735-5043
service@multiculbv.com
www.multiculbv.com

Applause Learning
Resources
85 Fernwood Lane
Roslyn, NY 11576-1431
(516) 365-1259
(800) APPLAUSE
Toll Free Fax
(877) 365-7484
www.applauselearning.
com

Sosnowski Language
Resources
58 Sears Rd.
Wayland, MA 01778
(508) 358-7891
Fax (508) 358-6687
sosnow@ma.ultranet.
com

Teacher's Discovery
2741 Paldan Dr.
Auburn Hills, MI 48326
(800) TEACHER
(248) 340-7210
Fax (248) 340-7212
www.teachersdiscovery.
com

Clarity Language
Consultants Ltd
(Hong Kong and UK)
PO Box 163, Sai Kung,
HONG KONG
Tel (+852) 2791 1787, Fax
(+852) 2791 6484
www.clarity.com.hk

SpeakWare
2836 Stephen Dr.
Richmond, CA 94803
(510) 222-2455
leds@speakware.com
www.speakware.com